DESERT EXILE

The Uprooting of a Japanese American Family

YOSHIKO UCHIDA

UNIVERSITY OF WASHINGTON PRESS

Seattle and London

In memory of my mother and father

and all the Issei

who were strong and of good courage

Portions of chapters 3 and 4 first appeared, in slightly altered form, in Yoshiko Uchida's "Evacuation: The First Five Months," *California Monthly* 77 (November 1966). A much abridged excerpt from chapters 7 and 8 also appeared in her "Topaz, City of Dust," *Utah Historical Quarterly* 48 (Summer 1980).

Library of Congress Cataloging in Publication Data
Uchida, Yoshiko.
    Desert exile.
    1. Japanese Americans—Evacuation and relocation,
1942–1945. 2. Uchida, Yoshiko. 3. World War,
1939–1945—Personal narratives, American.
4. Japanese Americans—California—Biography.
5. California—Biography. I. Title.
D769.8.A6U25   940.54'72'73   81-16187
ISBN 0-295-95898-7   AACR2

Contents

Desert Exile

1. The House above Grove Street

Whenever I am in the neighborhood, I find myself drawn back to Stuart Street, to drive once more past the stucco bungalow just above Grove, where my older sister, Keiko, and I grew up.

I remember the sunny yard in back with the peach and apricot and fig trees. I remember the sweetpeas that grew higher than my head, and the enormous chrysanthemums that measured seventeen inches around. There was a blackberry bush that rambled wild along the back fence, and there was rhubarb that sprang up near the fenced enclosure where we kept a succession of three dogs. When we were little there were swings and a sandbox, and later a hammock my father had bought to console us when our first dog died of distemper.

I remember my father in his gardening clothes, raking the yard and filling the dusky evening air with the wonderful smell of burning leaves, and my mother standing at the back porch, wearing her big apron, ringing a small black bell because she didn't like calling out to bring us in for supper.

It was a sunny, pleasant three-bedroom house we rented, and there was nothing particularly unusual about our living there except that we were Japanese Americans.[1] And in those days before the Second World War, few Japanese families in Berkeley, California, lived above Grove Street with the exception of some early settlers. It seemed the realtors of the area had drawn an invisible line through the city and agreed

1. I use the term "Japanese American" to include the first generation immigrant Japanese, as well as the second and third generations.

among themselves not to rent or sell homes above that line to Asians. The finer homes in east Berkeley and on the hills overlooking San Francisco Bay belonged to another world into which we rarely ventured, except on our way to church to pick up a Japanese "school boy" or "school girl" who worked for a white family while attending the university.

I'm not sure how my father found a homeowner willing to ignore the realtors' tacit agreement and rent us the house on Stuart Street. I do know, however, how he handled an earlier difficulty when he and my mother rented their first home in Oakland in 1917.

Newly married, they had just furnished the house with carpets, curtains, and furniture, when three men who professed to represent "The Santa Fe Improvement Association" called on them. They came not to welcome my parents to the neighborhood, but to tell them to get out.

"Can you tell me who complained about us?" my father asked.

"The members of the association," the men answered.

My father had just joined the San Francisco branch of Mitsui and Company, one of Japan's major import-export firms, where he eventually became assistant manager. He gave the men one of his business cards and informed them the owner of the house had assured him there would be no objection to my parents' presence in the neighborhood.

"I'd like to meet those members of your association who object to us," he told the men. "If they can bring proof that we are undesirable elements in this neighborhood, we will leave immediately. Otherwise I feel their request is unreasonable. How would you feel," he asked, "if you went to Tokyo and were treated like this?"

The men could not reply. "We only represent the other members," they explained lamely.

"Then send those members to me," my father insisted. "I would like to meet them face to face and get acquainted."

Those members never came and their three representatives never returned. My father had won, and my parents remained in the house, but it was only a small victory, for those were days of such intense anti-Asian sentiment, there were billboards bearing signs that read, "Japs, don't let the sun shine on you here. Keep moving."

Although such racism had not abated by the time my parents began to raise a family, my sister and I had a happy childhood, wrapped in the love and affection of our parents and in the gentle innocence of our environment. We grew up during the depression but were fortunate enough to be unaware of it, even though my parents were thrifty and self-denying, as they continued to be for their entire lives.

My father, Dwight Takashi Uchida, came to California in 1906 at the age of twenty-two, after having taught Japanese in a small school in Hawaii for about three years. He arrived on a small cargo boat and landed in San Francisco just three months after the great earthquake to find the tower of the ferry building still askew and Market Street piled high with ash.

He had hoped to go to Yale and eventually to become a doctor, but he went first to Seattle where his mother, having just lost a daughter to leukemia, had immigrated to be with another of her daughters. There he found work in a general merchandise store owned by a successful Japanese entrepreneur, M. Furuya, and abandoned his earlier ambitions. A year later he was sent to manage Furuya's Portland store where he stayed for nine years, earning enough to send boat fare to his two remaining sisters in Japan, so they could join their mother in Seattle.

While he was manager of the Portland Furuya, it doubled in size and became one of the first Japanese stores to have a branch of the United States Post Office on its premises. It was as an employee of Furuya that my father learned to wear a white shirt and black bow tie every day, always to be punctual, and to answer the telephone before it rang twice. These habits became so thoroughly ingrained, they remained with him the rest of his life.

His work at Furuya brought him to the attention of the manager of the San Francisco branch of Mitsui and Company, and in 1917 he went to San Francisco to become one of its employees. In the same year he married Iku Umegaki, who had come from Japan the previous year to marry him.

They had never met, but had corresponded for over a year at the suggestion of professors who knew them both while they were students at Doshisha University in Kyoto, one of Japan's foremost Christian universities.

It seems incredible to me that my mother—a shy, reticent, and sheltered woman—could have taken so enormous a leap across the Pacific Ocean, leaving behind her family and friends and all that was dear to her. And yet many Japanese women did the same in those days. I believe those early Issei (first generation Japanese immigrant) women must have had tremendous reserves of strength and courage to do what they did, often masked by their quiet and unassertive demeanor. They came to an alien land, created homes for their men, worked beside them in fields, small shops, and businesses, and at the same time bore most of the responsibility for raising their children. Theirs was a determination and endurance born, I would say, of an uncommon spirit.

My mother was twenty-four when she came to the United States and was the eldest of five children. Her father, once a samurai, had been a prefectural governor, but died when my mother was twelve. It was a harsh struggle for her mother to raise five children alone, and it became necessary for her to send the youngest boy to a temple to be raised as a priest, although some years later she herself became a Christian.

My mother worked for her room, board, and tuition at Doshisha University and also did such chores as mending and ironing for some of her American missionary instructors. Her favorite teacher once asked her to embroider two and a half yards of scallops around one of her petticoats. It was a task my mother could accomplish only by staying up every night long after all the other girls had gone to bed and working for many hours beside the small light left burning in her dormitory. And it was only after several weeks that she finally finished the tedious chore. In those early years, there existed such a close bond between student and teacher, and my mother's admiration for her teachers was so great, that rather than feeling exploited she considered it a privilege to work for them.

It was the same respect and trust that led her to come to America to marry my father, following the advice of the Japanese professors who knew both my parents and urged their union.

I imagine her decision to leave Japan was a much more difficult one than my father's, for while he came to join his mother and sister, she had no one except him. She left behind her mother, three brothers, and a sister, and the day she sailed she cried until her eyes were so

My father (left) with two college friends.
Kyoto, Japan, about 1902.

My father with his mother (center front) and four sisters. Japan,
about 1902.

My mother on her graduation from Doshisha University.
She stands between two of her favorite instructors, both of
whom remained lifelong friends. Kyoto, Japan, 1914.

swollen she could scarcely see. I know how much my mother must have missed her family in Japan, but I also know she never regretted having come to America to marry my father.

Because my father was a salaried man at Mitsui, our lives were more secure and somewhat different from many of our Japanese friends, especially those whom we knew at the small Japanese church we attended. For them life in the 1930s was a dark desperate struggle for survival in a country where they could neither become citizens nor own land. Many spoke little English. Some of the mothers took in sewing or did day work in white homes. Others operated home laundries, washing clothes in damp cold basements, drying them on ropes strung across musty attics, and pressing them with irons heated on the kitchen stove. Most of the fathers struggled to keep open such small businesses as dry cleaners, laundries, groceries, or shoe repair shops, and they sometimes came to ask my father for advice and help.

My father understood their struggles well, for he too had grown up in poverty in Japan. His father, a former samurai turned teacher, had died when he was ten. His mother, married at sixteen and widowed at thirty, sent her five children to live with various relatives, and my father never forgot the sadness of those long snow-covered roads he walked to reach the home of the uncle who took him in.

His mother went to Kyoto to work as a housekeeper in the home of American missionaries who taught at Doshisha University and was converted by them to Christianity. My father was later given the name of the master of the household, Dwight.

His mother saved every yen she earned and was eventually able to call her children, one by one, to live with her in a small house at the rear of her employer's home. Often all they had for supper was rice and *daikon* (long white radish). "There were days when the *daikon* tasted especially good," my father used to recall, "and that was when my mother had cooked it with the liquid she'd saved from the canned salmon eaten by the white folks."

My father worked his way through Doshisha University by delivering milk in the mornings, working as a telephone operator at night, and later serving as a clerk in a bank.

Because both my parents had learned to be frugal in their youth and had worked hard for a living, they were never wasteful or self-indulgent even when they had the means. They also felt much compassion for anyone in need. When one of our neighbors on Stuart Street lost his job during the depression, and his wife sold homemade bread, my mother not only bought her bread, but arranged to learn French from her as well, to give her the additional income. I remember my mother waking us in those days calling, *"Levez-vous,* Kei Chan, Yo Chan! *Levez-vous!"*

My parents also provided solace and frequent meals to lonely homesick students from Japan who were studying at the University of California or the Pacific School of Religion. These students seemed to come to our home in an unending procession, much to the dismay of my sister and I who found them inordinately dull. They came pressed and polished in their squeaky shoes, their hair slicked down with camellia hair oil whose sharp sweet scent I identified as the smell of Japan. They crowded around our table on most holidays, on frequent Sundays, and they often dropped in uninvited for a cup of tea.

These students were only part of the deluge from Japan. There were also visiting ministers, countless alumni from Doshisha University, and sometimes the president of the university himself. I felt as though our house was the unofficial alumni headquarters for Doshisha and I one of its most reluctant members.

Some of the Japanese ministers who visited us were humble and kind, but others were pompous and pedantic. One could sing all the books of the Bible to the tune of a folk song, while another left his dirty bath water in the tub for my mother to wash out. Most of them stayed too long, I thought, and talked too much.

These importunate callers, it seemed to me, were intrusive and boring, not only causing my mother to work long hours in the kitchen, but depriving me on occasion of her attention.

There was the time I came home from school bursting with news. "Mama, I found a dead sparrow! Come help me give it a funeral!" But Mama was imprisoned in the living room over a tray of tea, as she so often was, entertaining a visitor from Japan.

There was one frequent caller, a seminary student, who would come on cold wintry days and spend long silent hours sitting by our fireplace. My mother gave up trying to engage him in conversation and usually sat opposite him knitting or crocheting.

I would cast hateful glances at him through the crack at the kitchen door, hearing the sputtering of the oak logs and my mother's occasional sighs. More than once I tried to be rid of him by standing a broom upside down in the kitchen and covering its bristles with a dustcloth. This was an old Japanese belief, my mother had once told me, that would cause unwanted visitors to leave. Sometimes it worked, and sometimes it didn't. But the time I set up the broom at the crack of the doorway, the somber seminarian left immediately. In my great and utter delight, it never once occurred to me that our visitor might have known a few old Japanese beliefs himself.

My father had a permanent dock pass that enabled him to board the ships of the Nippon Yusen Company when they berthed in San Francisco, and he often spent hours shepherding visitors from Japan through customs, showing them the sights of the city, and then driving them to our house for dinner. He thrived on company and welcomed these opportunities. But my sister and I complained shamelessly.

"Company again?" we would groan. "Those people from the seminary again?" we would object.

But we knew all the proper motions required to help prepare for a dinner. We would flutter dust cloths over the furniture, pull open the dining room table to add extra boards, get out my mother's white linen tablecloth and napkins, and set the table with her good silverplate service. If we felt particularly helpful, we would pick nasturtiums or sweetpeas from the backyard and stuff them in the hollow back of a china swan for the centerpiece. If it was close to a holiday, we would try to have appropriate decorations, and I loved the delicate silver deer that grazed on our mirror centerpiece at Christmas time.

In spite of our grumbling, sometimes my sister and I enjoyed ourselves. Both my parents had a lively sense of humor, and there was often much laughter as well as after dinner singing at our parties. We sang everything from "Old Black Joe" to "In the Good Old Summertime."

Sometimes Keiko and I would have our own private jokes that would trigger such a spate of giggles one of us would have to leave the table. At one of our dinners, a very serious bespectacled seminarian suddenly rose from the table in the middle of dinner and disappeared for

One of our early portraits taken in Berkeley when I was about three and my
sister about seven.

several minutes into the kitchen. When he returned to the table he seemed much happier.

"It was so warm, I took the liberty of removing an extra pair of wool underwear," he explained rather sheepishly. "I feel much better now."

My sister and I exchanged a quick glance, before both of us rushed into the kitchen to explode in helpless laughter, and it was quite a while before either of us could go back again to the dinner table.

We had another group of guests, more sophisticated and worldly, who were my father's associates at Mitsui. They were the "Company people" sent from Japan to live and work temporarily in the United States. They drank and smoked, neither of which my father did, and knew little of the depression or the anxieties of the Japanese who had immigrated to this country. My father played golf with the men, and my mother entertained their well-dressed ladies at teas.

She also invited them to elaborate dinners in our home. Sometimes my father would cook sukiyaki at the table on a small cooker with gas piped in from our stove. He would begin with thick white chunks of suet, add thin slices of beef, then onions, scallions, bamboo shoots, mushrooms, tofu (bean curd cake), and other vegetables, all of which my mother had sliced and arranged carefully on enormous serving platters. By the time he added soy sauce, sugar, and saké, the wonderful aroma that filled our house was almost unbearable. At other times my mother would serve a totally Western meal, beginning with shrimp cocktail, olives, and celery, then some sort of roast with vegetables, and usually topped off with one of her famous banana cream cakes.

We in turn were invited to their homes and to the manager's mansion in San Francisco each year for a fancy Christmas party. But I never felt comfortable with these people. Their "haut monde" outlook, far removed from our own simple life style made me ill at ease. On the other hand, we didn't seem to fit in with the group that comprised our Sunday world either, and I felt constrained with them in a totally different way. My mother, sensitive and empathic, felt guilty that circumstances enabled us to live in comfort when life for them was so difficult, and she was always careful to restrain us in both dress and behavior on Sundays.

My sister and I never lacked for clothing, as my mother sewed most of our dresses herself. Her years of apprenticeship at Doshisha, sewing and embroidering for her teachers, had served her well, and now she lavished the same care and attention on her own children. Our dresses were detailed with fine tucks, smocking, hemstitching, rows of tiny mother-of-pearl buttons, and the most meticulous of hand finished touches.

I still remember the white pongee dresses with red and blue belts that she made for us to wear to the Olympic Games. And there were the flowered voiles with matching capes and hand-rolled hems, a blue one for Keiko and a red one for me. We must have begged to be allowed to wear them to Sunday School, but our delicious joy in our finery was tempered by our awareness that our friends in Sunday School couldn't have as many nice things as we had.

My mother was a giving and deeply caring person. "Don't ever be indifferent," she used to say to us. "Indifference is the worst fault of all." And she herself was never indifferent. She cared and felt deeply about everything around her. She could find joy in a drive to the park, a rainbow in the sky, a slim new moon, or an interesting weed appearing among the irises. She so empathized with anyone in distress that on one occasion she sent herbs to a diabetic man she had just met in the dentist's waiting room.

There was seldom a gift to our family that she and my father didn't share if they could. Whenever we received a crate of oranges or avocados or fresh vegetables from friends in the country, they would immediately distribute at least half the bounty to our neighbors and friends. But Keiko and I sometimes found it hard to share their generosity. "Don't give it *all* away," we would cry out. "Leave some for *us!*"

My mother's handiwork, too, was not confined just to our family. She embroidered fancy guest towels for many of her friends, and she must have made at least a hundred baby booties over the years for all the babies born into our church community.

Because she was also an excellent cook, her giving often took the form of food. She used to bake dozens of cream puffs sprinkled with powdered sugar and take them to anyone who was in need of cheer. Sometimes she made an enormous bowl of *chirashi-zushi* (a vinegared vegetable, chicken, and rice mixture) for us, but a platter was usually shared with a lonely friend. She spent many hours chopping and cooking the nine or ten ingredients and garnishes for it, and I would stand at the table and fan the steaming rice for her to hasten its cooling before everything could be mixed together. *Chirashi-zushi* was one of my favorite dishes, and Mama usually made it for me on my birthday as an added gift.

Most of her Saturday nights seemed to be taken up with cooking as she prepared large quantities of food for our Sunday guests. Long after I had gone to bed, I would hear her knife chattering on the cutting board, and I would drift off to sleep with delicious aromas swirling around my head. Mama's cooking was as meticulous as her sewing. She carefully removed every bruise on vegetables, washed them with great care, and then cooked from the heart. It was no wonder everybody loved to come have dinner with us.

In spite of the time they devoted to other people, my parents managed to enrich our lives in many ways. They took my sister and me almost everywhere they went—to visit friends, to church, to occasional operas or theatrical performances, to the Legion of Honor and the de Young museums in San Francisco, and to concerts to hear such luminaries as Ignace Jan Paderewski and Mme. Ernestine Schumann-Heink. It was probably my mother's interest in art that led us to the museums and my father's love of music that took us to the concerts. I recall liking best the Cossacks' Chorus, whose ebullient singing so impressed me, I thought theirs was the finest concert I had ever heard.

My father loved to sing and never lost an opportunity to gather our friends around the piano for some dubious harmony in which he sang bass. He organized a choir for the young people at church, and he sang frequent solos at the service, although I don't know whether he was asked to do so, or simply volunteered in his usual forthright manner.

My sister and I both took piano lessons, and Keiko did the accompanying when we sang at home. Practicing piano was one of my more painful chores, however, and there were times when I never took the music out of my case from one lesson to the next. I must have been a great trial to my piano teacher, a gracious southern woman who never once showed the impatience she must have felt with me.

The four of us usually did everything together as a family, including going to the movies. Those were days when the theaters gave away dinnerware and prizes to entice people to come, and one night Papa had the lucky stub and won a prize. He strode up to the stage, bowed to the manager as he accepted his prize, and waved to the audience with what I thought was remarkable aplomb.

There were other times when Mama, Keiko, and I had our own special outings. Sometimes we would take the streetcar on Grove Street and go downtown to Oakland to shop. Mama carried a small brown satchel for her purchases and we would visit two or three department stores. I don't recall what my mother bought, but more important for me was our stop at the store restaurant where I always had a toasted ham sandwich and a chocolate ice cream soda. The snack itself was a special treat, but equally pleasant was having some private fun without fear of having an unwanted visitor arrive to spoil it by taking up Mama's time.

My father's railroad pass enabled us to take many trips, and each New Year's we took the Southern Pacific overnight sleeper to Los Angeles to spend the holiday with my paternal grandmother who lived with my aunt, uncle, and six cousins. Although there were five adults and eight children crammed into a small bungalow with only one bathroom, my cousins obligingly doubled up and we somehow managed and had great times together.

I believe we were among the few Nisei (second generation Japanese) who had even one grandparent living in the United States, and I feel fortunate to have known the spirited woman that my grandmother, Katsu Uchida, was.

She was a devout Christian from the days of her conversion in Kyoto, and as busy as she was helping care for the house and children (my aunt was a semi-invalid for many years), she found time to read her Japanese Bible every day. God was, for her, an intimate friend and she spent at least thirty minutes every night sitting on her bed, her legs folded beneath her, her eyes shut tight, rocking back and forth as she poured out her supplications and gratitude to Him.

Her early years of hardship in Japan had instilled in her a vigorous frugality, and she saw to it that no food was ever wasted. We never ate the best of the fruits or vegetables, but ate those that were spoiling first. She had little interest in material possessions and most of the money my father sent her each month was contributed to her Japanese church on various occasions. She had only a few clothes hanging in her closet, and in her later years she pinned a note to her best black dress that read, "This is for my trip to Heaven."

My grandmother (we called her *Obah San*) often suffered from back and shoulder aches, and one of the tasks of my younger cousins was to burn bits of moxa at certain muscle points, first identified by a professional, on her back.

I remember seeing her sitting on a cushion on the floor, pinching out tiny cones of the soft downy moxa which my cousins would then place on her back. They would light the moxa with a stick of burning incense, watch the red glow flicker down the small cone, then brush the ash away with a long feather before applying the next cone. During the treatment, she had a continuous series of moxa cones smoldering on her back, and often at the same time she herself would apply other cones to her leg muscles.

The process sometimes took almost an hour, and I remember how the small room in which she sat was filled with the smoky scent of the burning incense and moxa, and the sounds of my grandmother sucking in her breath in pain.

Moxibustion (*okyu*, it was called) was commonly used in Japan as a counterirritant for various aches and pains, and my parents in their later years also used it from time to time. My mother especially found it helpful for her own back and shoulder pains.

New Year's was a special time in the early Issei households, for in Japan it is considered a time of renewal and new beginnings. Houses were cleaned, outstanding bills were paid before year's end, and a fresh start made in life. It was a time of joyous celebration and vast amounts of special holiday dishes were prepared.

We began our New Year's meal in Los Angeles with bowls of hot broth and toasted rice cakes. In the center of the long table was a whole broiled lobster, bright and colorful, symbolizing long life. There were tiered lacquer boxes filled with shredded *daikon* and sesame seed salad, sweetened black beans and lima beans (for good health), knots of seaweed (which I loved), and herring roe (which I could have done without). There were great platters filled with chicken, bamboo shoots, carrots, burdock, taro and lotus root, and hardboiled eggs cut into fancy shapes. Most of the dishes had special symbolism and were prepared over several days.

There was a strong sense of family at these three-generational gatherings and to commemorate the occasion we often had a two-family portrait taken.

The Issei had a great propensity for taking formal photographs to commemorate occasions ranging from birthdays and organizational get-togethers to weddings and even funerals. I suppose this was the only way they could share the event with their families and friends in Japan, but it also resulted in many bulging albums in our households. We had family portraits of all our relatives, most of my parents' friends and their families, and snapshots of every visitor who ever came to our house. Before we sat down to any of our company dinners, Papa always lined everybody up outside on our front lawn and took several snapshots with a succession of cameras from a Brownie box camera to a German Rolleiflex.

At one of our Los Angeles gatherings, because there were thirteen of us for our portrait, my mother suggested we include a doll as a fourteenth presence. Despite her efforts to ward off bad luck, however, two of my cousins died too young and too early—one a victim of the war while he was in Japan, and the other succumbing to a heart condition aggravated by her forced move to the Heart Mountain camp during World War II. In addition, my uncle became blind due to improper care following cataract surgery while interned in the same camp.

My father's railroad pass also enabled our family to take a long and memorable trip one summer that combined his business with our pleasure. We saw the Grand Canyon, New Orleans and its fabled French Quarter, and the great Mississippi River, which our train crossed by barge. I was so impressed by the sight of the magnificent river, I felt I had to do something and finally leaned over the barge railing and spit into the river to put a part of myself forever into its deep waters.

We visited several eastern cities, but most important to my mother was a special trip we made to the small village of Cornwall, Connecticut, to visit one of her former Doshisha instructors (the one whose petticoat she had embroidered) and to meet for the first time two white women pen pals with whom she had corresponded since college. Both my mother and father were great letter writers and kept up a voluminous correspondence. They cherished their many friends and I don't believe either of them ever lost one for neglect on their part.

We were probably the first Asians ever to visit Cornwall and one of its residents, an elderly white woman, patted me on the head and said, "My, but you speak English so beautifully." She had looked at my Japanese face and addressed only my outer person, and although she had meant to compliment me, I was thoroughly abashed to be perceived as a foreigner. On the other hand, I also met a lovely auburn-haired young girl named Cathy and began a friendship and correspondence with her that was to last a lifetime.

When I was about twelve and my sister sixteen, we took another major trip, this time to Japan, and our Los Angeles grandmother came with us. Our ship, the *Chichibu Maru*, took a leisurely two weeks to cross the Pacific, and unlike the crowded and foul smelling one-class ships on which my parents had come to America, this liner was quite luxurious.

My mother recalled how, on the small ship that brought her to this country, she had been served a sweet bean dessert in a bowl still reeking of the morning's fish soup. This time we were able to travel first class, and for me the costume parties, the sukiyaki parties on deck, and the bountiful afternoon teas were far more enjoyable than anything I encountered once I was in Japan.

For my parents, of course, it was a joyous time of homecoming. I remember when my mother, looking out the porthole of our cabin, first caught sight of her own mother waiting for her on the crowded pier below. "*Oka San*! Mother!" she cried out in a voice I had never heard before. Although she had made one earlier visit to Japan, she was seeing her mother for the first time in over ten years, and her cry held as much anguish over the long years of separation as her deep joy in seeing her once more. I think that moment when I heard her cry was my first perception of my mother as a person, with her own feelings as a daughter, and not just as a mother to me.

For my sister and me, the long drawn-out visits with my parents' friends, with uncles, aunts, and cousins who were total strangers, were often boring and dull, for although we understood some Japanese, many of the conversations were beyond our comprehension. I occasionally amused myself by counting the number of times my parents exchanged bows with their friends during a single visit, and I think the most was thirteen times.

For my grandmother, the homecoming must have held special meaning I could scarcely understand then, for she was returning to her homeland where once she had struggled so hard to exist, accompanied this time by her devoted son, now a successful businessman in the United States.

My father was indeed a businessman in every sense. He was practical and pragmatic, and possessed tremendous energy, enthusiasm, and a joyful eagerness to accomplish successfully any endeavor he undertook. He did everything quickly, from working, to eating, to walking. He was always in a hurry to get wherever he was going and, once there, left promptly when his mission was accomplished. My mother, on the other hand, was exactly the opposite, and I think she found it difficult to feel constantly rushed by Papa. Being a Japanese woman, however, she behaved as a Japanese wife, and adjusted even to having Papa stride several paces ahead of her, not from arrogance, but from impatience. For many years she sat in the back seat of the car, too self-conscious to take the seat up in front beside my father. It is possible, however, that she felt safer there, for Papa was a terrible driver, and caused Mama to clutch frequently at whoever sat next to her, calling out, "Be careful, Papa San! Be careful!"

Papa often went sailing through intersections without bothering to look both ways, and once, just two blocks from home, we were struck so hard by another car (the only other one in sight) that it turned ours over on its side. My screams brought people rushing to help us, and we were all pulled out through one of the side windows, shaken but unhurt except for a few bumps and bruises. After that accident, poor Mama was more nervous than ever about riding in Papa's car.

My father was outspoken and so completely without guile that he often blurted out remarks that would make my mother cringe. On seeing friends after an interval of many years, he might blithely tell them how much weight they had put on or how gray they had gotten, not with any meanness of spirit, but simply with complete candor.

I suspect his forthright manner caused some to be hurt and some even to resent him. But if this bothered Papa he never showed it. He had a sense of confidence that sprang from a strong self-image. He was Japanese and proud of his land and his heritage. Although both my parents loved America, they always held at the core of their being an abiding love for their native land.

If my father was sometimes too candid, he was also thoughtful and tender at heart. It was he who recorded in English the entries in my Baby Book with the flowing graceful hand he had learned at night school, although my mother inserted her own special message on the page with the tiny envelope containing wisps of hair from my first haircut. He never came home from a business trip without some little gift for each of us. He put much time and thought into looking for these special gifts—a silver pin from Jensen's in New York for Mama, a bejeweled flower pin or silver charm bracelet for Keiko and me. We didn't always appreciate his taste in jewelry, but we knew he loved us and had thought of us on his trip. My sister even now has a gold ring with her birthstone which my father presented to my mother when Keiko was born, and he often brought a bouquet of freesias to my mother in remembrance of the March birthday of their firstborn.

My mother was a dreamer—a gentle, sensitive, and creative person who, when she found time for her own interests, wrote many *tanka* (thirty-one syllable Japanese poems) using the pen name Yukari.[1] She felt too humble about her poems to have them appear in anything other than the Japanese Women's Christian Temperance Union periodical published by one of her close friends, but many found her *tanka*

1. Those of her poems included in this book are my translations from the original Japanese. Since there is a great loss of grace and nuance when rendering *tanka* into English, I have tried only to capture the spirit of her poems.

beautiful and moving. After her death, my father and I collected as many of her poems as we could, some written on scraps of paper or on the backs of envelopes, and had them published in book form in Japan.

Mama loved to read and owned dozens of books, including the Japanese translation of Tolstoy's entire works which she had hoped one day to read, but never did. Her bureau was always piled high with periodicals and books, but they too usually went unread. As she grew older, she put aside a half hour each morning to read, but it was only the Bible she found time for.

She was studious by nature and kept many notebooks of new English words she had learned or of quotations she liked. Unable to part with her college notebooks, she brought most of them with her to America in her big brown trunk, along with the books she had read in her English literature courses at Doshisha. I still have one of her notebooks, the ink now faded to the color of dust, in which she copied with the precise hand learned from her missionary teachers quotations from Bacon, Milton, Tagore, and Eliot and poems by Longfellow, Browning, and Shelley. When she was in her seventies, she memorized again Wordsworth's "Daffodils" because, she said, she wanted to keep her mind alert.

On rare occasions when time permitted, she would get out her writing box, rub the stick of *sumi* on the inkstone, and paint or practice calligraphy on a sheet of soft rice paper that had come wrapped around a gift from Japan.

But most of the time, my mother's own dreams and creative pursuits, pushed aside for the needs and demands of her family, existed only in bits and pieces on the fringes of her life.

The two of them, my mother and father, complemented each other well. My father enjoyed working with figures and was extremely adept at using the abacus. He checked the monthly bills from the Japanese grocer, kept all the accounts, and never allowed a bill to remain unpaid on his desk for more than a day or two.

My mother, on the other hand, was quite indifferent to money matters, seldom counted her change, and never wrote more than a handful of checks in her lifetime.

My dreamer mother instilled in my businessman father an appreciation of the creative aspects of life that sometimes escaped him, and brought out the tenderness close to the surface in him as well. He came to love plants and flowers, and enjoyed growing them especially for the pleasure they gave my mother. He would often come in from the garden carrying a particularly beautiful flower saying, "Here, Mama, I dedicate this to you." And she would smile and say, "Thank you, Papa San," and put it in her best cut-glass vase.

In later years, my father also wrote some *tanka,* and although he was not as skilled as my mother at the craft, he learned to share that pleasure with her as well. Throughout their life, they always shared a deep and abiding faith that was the foundation of their marriage and of our life as a family as well.

Their marriage was an arranged one, as was the custom of their day. But I have always thought the professors who planned the match must surely have taken great pride in the glorious success of their endeavor.

Pale smoke rises
From the leaves I burn,
The sight of my mother
I see in myself.

I leave the path
To tread the fallen leaves,
And find in myself still
The heart of a child.

Misty memories
Of Kyoto festivals
Drift through my evening kitchen
With the fragrance of **fuki**.

Yukari

2. On Being Japanese and American

꠸ "Mama, bring me my umbrella if it rains."

"I will, Yo Chan, don't worry. Now be careful crossing the street."

Even when the sky was blue and the sun was out, Mama and I completed this ritual in Japanese every day. Only then did I trudge off to grammar school, secure in the knowledge that my mother would come if I needed her. And she would stand at the doorway in her apron, waving until she could no longer see me.

Perhaps my insecurity stemmed from being four years younger than my sister—a seemingly insurmountable gap in childhood. My sister was the tomboy of the family. She was bold and a daredevil, while I was cautious and careful, and I did everything she told me to.

It seemed to me she could do everything better than I, from roller skating to playing the piano, and later, to dancing and driving. But to her, I seemed to be the one who garnered most of the attention and affection of my parents and their friends because I was the youngest. Keiko and I played well together most of the time, but we also had some good fights and once she chased me around the house with a hairbrush. She could also exercise almost total control over me by saying the magic words, "all right for you," although I was never sure what they actually meant.

"Don't you tell Mama," she would threaten, "or all right for you." And my lips were sealed forever.

By the time we were in college, we were good friends and have been very close ever since. But I still suffer from the "little sister syndrome" and even now seek her advice about many things.

One thing we had in common even in our childhood, however, was being Nisei—the one aspect of our selves that made us different from our white classmates. Perhaps it was the constant sense of not being as good as the *hakujin* (white people), as well as being younger, that caused me to seek my mother's reassurance each morning. No matter what happened to me at school or anywhere else, I had to know Mama was always there for me.

Although our home was distinctly Japanese in mood, character, and structure as compared to those of our white classmates, my parents were not strict traditionalists. Their close contact at Doshisha with white people who were both friends and instructors had cultivated in both of them a more Western outlook than that possessed by many of the Japanese who immigrated to this country. As a result, our up-bringing was less strict than that of some of my Nisei friends.

The dominant language in our home, however, was Japanese. My parents spoke it to one another, to most of their friends and to my sister and me. But both understood us when my sister or I answered in English, and they had many non-Japanese friends with whom they conversed in English. There were days, however, when my mother would say to her friends, "I'm so sorry, but my English just won't come out today," and she struggled then, just as I do now with my fading Japanese.

Most of my father's business at Mitsui was conducted in English, and he always read the *San Francisco Chronicle* on the ferry or the Southern Pacific trains that took him to his office in San Francisco. The English language periodicals I recall in our house were the old *Literary Digest,* and later, *National Geographic, Reader's Digest, Life,* and the *Christian Century,* which my father read from cover to cover. But there were also dozens of books and magazines that came from Japan, and my parents never missed reading both copies of the local Japanese newspapers.

When we were young, most of the stories my mother read to my sister and me were Japanese folktales or children's stories from books she had ordered from Japan. She and my father also taught us many Japanese children's songs, and at night when Mama came in to say our prayers with us, she always prayed in Japanese. Long after I became an adult, when it came to praying, I found it more natural to use my mother's native tongue.

There were also certain Japanese phrases that were an integral part of our daily lives. We never began a meal without first saying to my mother, *"Itadaki masu"* (a gracious acknowledgment to a hostess or whoever prepared the meal), and *"Gochiso sama"* (a sort of thanks for the fine food) when we had finished eating. I still long to say these words when I am a dinner guest, and indeed do so when I am at my sister's or at another Nisei home. *"Itte maeri masu"* (I'm leaving now) and *"Tadaima"* (an abbreviated version of I'm home now) were also two Japanese phrases my sister and I called out almost every day of our young lives.

Our daily meals, in contrast to our company dinners, consisted of simple fare, and were often a mixture of East and West. We always had rice instead of potatoes, however, and used soy sauce on our meat and fish rather than gravies and sauces.

My father, a hearty eater, could easily consume three or four bowls of rice for supper, and he had a portly figure as evidence of his appetite. No matter what we had for supper, however, he usually ended his meal with *ochazuké*—hot tea poured over a bowl of rice and eaten with whatever pickled vegetable my mother had in her large pickling bin. He had grown up on *ochazuké* in Japan, and my sister and I, too, grew up with an appreciation and taste for its simple honest flavors.

No Issei woman I knew could drive, and my mother was no exception. Most of our food was ordered by telephone from a small Japanese grocery shop and a boy delivered it with a bill written entirely in Japanese. It was probably just as well that my mother never went there in person, for its casual attitude toward sanitation might well have caused her to abandon it completely.

She was almost obsessive about cleanliness and always carried in her purse a small metal case she had brought with her from Japan. In it she kept small wads of cotton soaked in alcohol with which Keiko and I wiped fingers if we couldn't wash our hands before eating out.

Also in her purse was a packet of Japanese face powder that came in sheets inside a tiny booklet. Although my mother seldom used cosmetics and only waved her hair with a curling iron heated on the stove, she did remove the shine from her face on occasion by tearing a page from her powder booklet and rubbing it over her forehead and nose.

Her purse was a storehouse of Japanese sundries. Besides a tiny Japanese sewing kit, there was also a small bottle of pills that looked like tiny golden poppy seeds. We called them *"Kinbon San,"* and I am not sure what they contained, but they were a good cure-all and Mama believed in them just as she did in the healthful properties of celery phosphate.

I was never very robust. I got carsick and seasick. I developed sudden temperatures that were no doubt psychosomatic, occurring as they did just before a trip. I had nose bleeds that terrified me (I thought they would never stop), and my knees ached from "growing pains" that I assumed were the price of growing tall. It seems patently unfair that after enduring so many knee aches, I ended up not quite five feet tall. My mother sometimes tried to ease my discomfort with her "hot hands," a "gift" passed on to her by a Japanese friend. She would rub her palms together vigorously, hold them awhile as in prayer, and when she felt energy vibrating in her hands, she would apply them to my knees. If that didn't help, there was always the magical *"Kinbon San."*

Because she was not robust either, my mother was easy prey for any salesman who came offering hope for better health. She once bought a strange contraption made in Japan which I think was called an "Ox-Healer." It consisted of strands of wire issuing from a small box that probably contained a battery. The wires were attached to the body at the wrists and ankles with small metal plates, and one day I was entangled in them during an illness when the school nurse came to see me. Although I was willing to submit in solitude to my mother's Japanese ministrations, I was not about to have the school nurse catch me enmeshed in this strange contraption. With some wild thrashing I was able to extricate myself and managed to shove the wires to the foot of the bed just as the nurse walked into the room.

The "Ox-Healer" salesman was just one of many who came to our house, and my mother seldom turned away anyone who needed to make a living by selling things from door to door. This might very well have been because in Japan she had been accustomed to purchasing many items, from groceries to charcoal, from peddlers who called at the back door.

She befriended the Realsilk saleswoman who came with a bulging black bag of silken samples, and not only ordered hosiery and silk underwear from her, but always served her tea and cakes as she would to a friend. She also bought bottles of vanilla and lemon extract from the Watkins man, ordered mops and furniture wax from the Fuller Brush man, and purchased Wearever pans from a Japanese salesman. Once she bought a set of music books which she thought would be a fine addition to our *Book of Knowledge* set and might also encourage my sister and me to practice more between piano lessons.

My father never questioned her smaller indulgences, but the music books proved to be another matter. They involved a sizable sum of money, and he informed Mama quite firmly that in the future he was to be consulted before she made any major purchases. I don't think it was the money that bothered Papa as much as the fact that he felt his role as head of the house had been diminished by my mother's impulsive purchase.

Those were days when the cleaners still picked up and delivered clothes on wood hangers and the People's Bread man came by in a wagon filled with buttery pastries and fresh baked bread. Buying a service or a product then meant dealing with a pleasant human being rather than dropping a coin in a slot or picking out a prepackaged item in a giant supermarket, and my mother thought of all these people as her friends.

Besides the paintings, pottery, and other Japanese works of art in our home, there were certain Japanese customs that we observed regularly. Every year before March 3 (Dolls Festival Day), my mother, sister, and I would open the big brown trunk that had come with Mama from Japan. From its depths we would extract dozens and dozens of small wooden boxes containing the tiny ornamental dolls she had collected over the years. They were not the usual formal set of Imperial Court dolls normally displayed for this festival, but to me they were much more appealing.

My mother's vast and rambling collection included rural folk toys and charms, dolls of eggshell and corn husks, dolls representing famous Noh or Kabuki dances or characters in the folktales she had read to us, miniature dishes and kitchen utensils, and even some of the dolls she had played with as a child herself. It took well over an hour for us to open the boxes and put the collection out for display, but to Mama each doll was like an old friend. "My, how nice to see you," she would say, welcoming their annual emergence, and she included the American dolls we played with at the foot of the display table so they wouldn't feel left out. She usually invited friends to tea to share the pleasure of seeing her dolls as well as the peach tree that accommodated by blossoming at the same time.

My mother put the dolls out faithfully each year until they were put in storage during the war. In later years, when she grew too old and the effort to display them was too great, she still opened her trunk, but took out only the Emperor and Empress dolls and bowed to the others relegated to remain in the darkness of the trunk.

"*Gomen nasai, neh,*" she would apologize. "I'm so sorry I can't take you all out this year," and she would pat the top of the trunk as she closed the lid in a small gesture of resignation and farewell.

Now it is I who find pleasure in getting the dolls out once a year from their small boxes of paulownia wood. But it is not so much in remembrance of Dolls Festival Day that I display them as in remembrance of my mother and her Japanese ways.

I also remember my parents on the anniversary day of their death by placing flowers beside their photograph, just as I had seen them do, perpetuating a Buddhist tradition that had been an intrinsic part of their early lives. The Issei were very close to their dead and their funerals were elaborate and lengthy affairs often attended by hundreds of people. In the early years, these funerals were held at night to accommodate those who worked and couldn't take time off during the day, but even today many of my Nisei friends, following the traditions of their parents, still hold funeral services at night and perpetuate the custom of giving *okoden* (monetary gifts) to the family of the deceased. Our parents' Japaneseness is still very much a part of us.

The Japanese Independent Congregational Church of Oakland (now Sycamore Congregational Church) played a major role in the life of our family. Founded in 1904 by a small group of Japanese students, it was one of the first Japanese churches in the United States to free itself of the denominational Mission Boards and become self-supporting and self-governing. In its early years it operated a dormitory that housed young Japanese students who worked as they studied at the university or the seminary. The church not only enhanced their spiritual life but also filled their need for an ethnic community. As the Issei began to marry and raise families, it continued to be a focal point in their lives, providing support and a sense of community. Indeed it was almost an extended family, with each member caring and concerned about the lives of the others.

My parents were among the earliest members of this Japanese church and never missed attending services on Sunday. Consequently, my sister and I never missed going to Sunday School unless we were sick.

While Keiko and I were still having our toast and steaming cups of cocoa on Sunday mornings, Mama would cook a large pot of rice to be eaten with the food she had prepared the night before. When it was cooked, she took it to her bed and bundled it up in a thick quilt to keep warm until we got home from church with a carload of people who had no place to go for Sunday dinner.

Sunday School began at 10:00 A.M., but we always left home at least an hour earlier, since my father was for many years its superintendent and my mother one of its teachers. On our way to church we would stop at four or five houses, picking up children here and there until our car spilled over with them.

The Sunday School service was conducted in English, and all the children met together in the chapel to sing hymns, reading the words from large cloth pages that hung from a metal stand. "Open your mouths," my father would encourage us. "Let me hear you sing as loud as you can!" And we would oblige by bellowing out, "Jesus loves me this I know, for the Bible tells me so . . . ."

After the short service, we branched out to our classes to absorb whatever edifying thoughts our teachers could put into our heads. I can still recite half the books of the Bible and I can even sing some of them to the tune taught me by the minister from Japan who visited us. But more than anything I learned in class, what clings to my memory like frost on my bones is how cold I was in church during winter.

My class usually met in the old wooden building behind the chapel

The congregation and Sunday School of the Japanese Independent
Congregational Church of Oakland, about 1928.

that had once been the church dormitory and which we called "the Back House." Its only provision for heat was a small fireplace that seldom had a fire, and I would sit on a wooden folding chair, bundled up in my winter coat, and shiver all through class.

The chapel was heated by a coal furnace stoked by the first man who arrived at church. It produced a weak vapor of heat through two floor grills, and we would huddle around them before the Sunday School services trying to catch any faint wisps of heat that might emerge. My mother usually took a comforter to church to wrap around her legs in winter, but even then, she would emerge from the services looking bleak and stiff.

The adult service was conducted entirely in Japanese and usually lasted well over an hour, as long hymns droned on and on to the accompaniment of a wheezing reed organ. The minister delivered lengthy sermons which my father admitted to finding extremely tedious. But he added to the length of the service himself since, as one of the deacons, he made the weekly announcements and, once he began talking, found it difficult to be brief.

It was the dreary lot of my sister and me, and anyone else waiting for parents, to amuse ourselves outside until the service ended. Sometimes we sat in our car and read mystery stories. Sometimes we played marbles on the slotted metal doormat, or invented games of our own, or threw pebbles in the slimy green fishpond in back.

Often I was sent inside to check on the progress of the adult service. "Go see if they're almost done," my sister would say, and I would obligingly tiptoe to the chapel hoping to hear the singing of the Doxology. Instead, when I peeked in through the crack at the doorway, I would see the meager congregation sitting silent and patient—the men on one side of the center aisle, the women on the other, all dressed in their Sunday black clothes. One or two would be drowsing, their heads slumped on their chests after a weary week of labor, the others looking solemn and sad. I used to wonder why the minister always sounded so angry and what our parents had done to warrant such castigation.

When at last the service ended, the congregation would slip out into the warmth of the sun, bowing and exchanging polite greetings. But still we were not released. My father would stay to count the offering and bolt the front door after everyone left. Sometimes he seemed more of a minister than the minister himself, and he gave much time to the church as it limped from one minister to another. He was among the first to offer help to a church family in crisis and always picked up the faithful few who went to the weekly prayer meetings. In later years, he sometimes wrote and mailed the weekly bulletins, cleaned the building, and even mended the aisle rug.

My mother, too, gave much of her time and energy to the church. For a number of years she was president of the Women's Society and she also undertook many silent, unseen chores, one of which was the laundering each week of the soiled roller towel that hung in the dingy church washroom. The children of the Sunday School usually left it in such filthy condition, I always used to shake my hands dry rather than use it. But my mother would take it home, soak it overnight in soap and disinfectant, and scrub it until it emerged as clean as the rest of her wash.

Some Sundays, instead of serving lunch at home, Mama would pack a picnic lunch and we would go to Lake Merritt Park after church, taking with us five or six students and an elderly bachelor who lived a solitary existence in "the Back House." We would spread our car blanket out on the grass and eat our rice balls and Japanese food on small red lacquer dishes, using black lacquer chopsticks. I always felt extremely self-conscious about eating Japanese food and using chopsticks in public, for curious passersby would often stare coldly at our unusual picnic fare. Still, I had to admit it tasted better than sandwiches, even the thin cucumber sandwiches Mama made for her teas.

On rare Sundays when we had no guests, we would sometimes stop on the way home to visit someone who hadn't been able to come to church. We once stopped to see a woman who had just taken a steaming sponge cake from the oven and insisted we have a slice. I still recall how wicked I felt to be indulging in cake before lunch, for I had always thought Sundays were meant to be days of deprivation, when even small enjoyments were to be denied. It wasn't until I was in high school that I dared go to a movie on a Sunday afternoon, and even then I was so consumed with guilt, I didn't enjoy it very much.

Our lives—my sister's and mine—were quite thoroughly infused with the customs, traditions, and values of our Japanese parents, whose own lives had been structured by the samurai code of loyalty, honor, self-discipline, and filial piety. Their lives also reflected a blend of Buddhist philosophy dominated by Christian faith. So it was that we grew up with a strong dose of the Protestant ethic coupled with a feeling of respect for our teachers and superiors; a high regard for such qualities as frugality, hard work, patience, diligence, courtesy, and loyalty; and a sense of responsibility and love, not only for our parents and family, but for our fellow man.

My parents' Japaneseness was never nationalistic in nature. They held the Imperial family in affectionate and respectful regard, as did all Japanese of their generation. But their first loyalty was always to their Christian God, not to the Emperor of Japan. And their loyalty and devotion to their adopted country was vigorous and strong. My father cherished copies of the Declaration of Independence, the Bill of Rights, and the Constitution of the United States, and on national holidays he hung with great pride an enormous American flag on our front porch, even though at the time, this country declared the first generation Japanese immigrants to be "aliens ineligible for citizenship."

Although my parents were permanent residents of the United States, they were never naturalized, even when it became possible by law in 1952. They attended classes and prepared themselves for the required tests, but when the time came, my mother was reluctant to go. At the time, Issei were being naturalized in great numbers at massive, impersonal ceremonies, and my mother couldn't make herself go, saying she didn't want to be a part of anything where human beings were treated like a herd of cattle.

She was as devoted to America as my father, but I think she sensed the dehumanizing nature of the mass naturalization ceremonies, and also felt deep down that by becoming an American citizen, she was abandoning her native land. I think she couldn't bear to give up that part of herself that was Japanese. And my father understood. He deferred to her feelings, and they both remained Japanese citizens for the rest of their lives.

In spite of the complete blending of Japanese qualities and values

We often had family portraits taken when my grandmother came to visit us from Los Angeles.

Our house on Stuart Street where we lived until our forced removal.

Left: I felt like a foreigner when I wore my kimono for a special school program. *Right:* Keiko and I with Laddie, whom we had to leave behind when we went to camp.

Our family with my grandmother on the day we sailed for a visit to Japan. Next to my mother is her close friend (second from left) who came to see us off.

My sister (waving) and I (bending), on a picnic with an uncle and cousin in Japan.

into our lives, neither my sister nor I, as children, ever considered ourselves anything other than Americans. At school we saluted the American flag and learned to become good citizens. All our teachers were white, as were many of our friends. Everything we read was in English, which was, of course, our native tongue.

Unlike many of our Nisei peers, my sister and I refused to go to Japanese language school, and our parents never compelled us to go. Instead, my mother tried to teach us Japanese at home every summer during vacation. We had many stormy sessions as Mama tried to inject a little knowledge of a difficult language into two very reluctant beings. Learning Japanese to us was just one more thing that would accentuate our "differentness," something we tried very hard to overcome in those days. And despite my mother's diligent efforts, we seldom progressed beyond the fourth or fifth grade *Japanese Reader,* for during the year we would regress so badly that each summer we would have to begin again at Book One or Two. Much to my present regret, I never got beyond the fifth grade *Reader.*

I think the first time I became acutely aware of the duality of my person and the fact that a choice in loyalties might be made, was when I went with my cousins in Los Angeles to an event at the Olympic Games. Dressed in my red, white, and blue outfit, I was cheering enthusiastically for the American team when I became aware that my cousins were cheering for the men from Japan. It wasn't that they were any less loyal to America than I, but simply that their upbringing in the tightly-knit Japanese American community of Los Angeles and their attendance at Japanese Language School had caused them to identify with the men who resembled them in appearance. But I was startled and puzzled by their action. As Japanese as I was in many ways, my feelings were those of an American and my loyalty was definitely to the United States.

As I approached adolescence, I wanted more than anything to be accepted as any other white American. Imbued with the melting pot mentality, I saw integration into white American society as the only way to overcome the sense of rejection I had experienced in so many areas of my life. The insolence of a clerk or a waiter, the petty arrogance of a bureaucrat, discrimination and denial at many establishments, exclusion from the social activities of my white classmates—all of these affected my sense of personal worth. They reinforced my feelings of inferiority and the self-effacement I had absorbed from the Japanese ways of my parents and made me reticent and cautious.

For many years I never spoke to a white person unless he or she spoke to me first. At one of my freshman classes at the university, I found myself sitting next to a white student I had known slightly at high school. I sat silent and tense, not even turning to look at her because I didn't want to speak first and be rebuffed. Finally, she turned to me and said, "Yoshi, aren't you going to speak to me?"

Only then did I dare smile, acknowledge her presence, and become the friendly self I wanted to be. Now, my closest friend for the past twenty years has been a white person, but if I had met him in college, I might never have spoken to him, and I probably would not have gone out with him.

When I was in junior high school, I was the only Japanese American to join the Girl Reserve unit at our school and was accepted within the group as an equal. On one occasion, however, we were to be photographed by the local newspaper, and I was among the girls to be included. The photographer casually tried to ease me out of the picture, but one of my white friends just as stubbornly insisted on keeping me in. I think I was finally included, but the realization of what the photographer was trying to do hurt me more than I ever admitted to anyone.

In high school, being different was an even greater hardship than in my younger years. In elementary school one of my teachers had singled out the Japanese American children in class to point to our uniformly high scholastic achievement. (I always worked hard to get A's.) But in high school, we were singled out by our white peers, not for praise, but for total exclusion from their social functions. There was nothing I could do about being left out, but I could take precautions to prevent being hurt in other ways. When I had outgrown my father's home haircuts and wanted to go to a beauty parlor, I telephoned first to ask if they would take me.

"Do you cut Japanese hair?"

"Can we come swim in the pool? We're Japanese."

"Will you rent us a house? Will the neighbors object?"

These were the kinds of questions we asked in order to avoid embarrassment and humiliation. We avoided the better shops and restaurants where we knew we would not be welcome. Once during my college years, when friends from Los Angeles came to visit, we decided to go dancing, as we occasionally did at the Los Angeles Palladium. But when we went to a ballroom in Oakland, we were turned away by the woman at the box office who simply said, "We don't think you people would like the kind of dancing we do here." That put enough of a damper on our spirits to make us head straight for home, too humiliated to go anywhere else to try to salvage the evening.

Society caused us to feel ashamed of something that should have made us feel proud. Instead of directing anger at the society that excluded and diminished us, such was the climate of the times and so low our self-esteem that many of us Nisei tried to reject our own Japaneseness and the Japanese ways of our parents. We were sometimes ashamed of the Issei in their shabby clothes, their rundown trucks and cars, their skin darkened from years of laboring in sun-parched fields, their inability to speak English, their habits, and the food they ate.

I would be embarrassed when my mother behaved in what seemed to me a non-American way. I would cringe when I was with her as she met a Japanese friend on the street and began a series of bows, speaking all the while in Japanese.

"Come on, Mama," I would interrupt, tugging at her sleeve. "Let's go," I would urge, trying to terminate the long exchange of amenities. I felt disgraced in public.

Once a friend from Livingston sent my parents some pickled *daikon*. It had arrived at the post office on a Sunday, but the odor it exuded was so pungent, and repugnant to the postal workers, that they called us to come immediately to pick it up. When the clerk handed the package to me at arm's length with a look of utter disgust, I was mortified beyond words.

Unhappy in high school, I couldn't wait to get out. I increased my class load, graduated in two and a half years, and entered the University of California in Berkeley when I was sixteen, immature and naive. There I found the alienation of the Nisei from the world of the white students even greater than in high school. Asians were not invited to join the sororities or fraternities, which at the time were a vital part of the campus structure. Most of the Nisei avoided general campus social events and joined instead the two Japanese American social clubs—the Japanese Women's Student Club and the Japanese Men's Student Club. We had our own dances, picnics, open houses, and special events in great abundance. These activities comprised my only social outlet and I had a wonderful time at them.

My parents enjoyed the company of young people and always came out to meet and talk with whoever came by to pick up my sister or me. (We had by now become Kay and Yo.)

"Where is your home town?" my father would often ask, and no matter where the young man was from—Brawley, Fresno, Guadalupe, Los Angeles, or wherever—Papa usually knew someone there because of his many friendships through the statewide federation of Japanese churches. He could keep us standing in the living room for quite a while carrying on a lively conversation, obviously having a fine time. Eventually he would ask, "Why don't you people start your dances earlier so you can get home earlier? Nine o'clock is a ridiculous time to begin anything." And at this point I would quickly interrupt with, "Oh Papa, for heaven's sake!" and steer my date out the door.

One of my sister's dates once caused my mother to paint a unique message on our front steps, which were worn, slippery, and down-right dangerous on a rainy night. When she learned that my sister's friend had said goodnight and then slipped on our steps and slid in-gloriously to the bottom, she took immediate action. She not only put black adhesive tape on the steps, she bought some white paint and printed the words, "Please watch your step," one word to a step. The trouble was, however, that she had begun at the bottom and worked her way up, so as our friends departed they read the puzzling message, "Step your watch please." Nobody ever slipped after that, and everybody left our house laughing.

All during my college years I dated only Nisei and never went out socially with a white man until many years after the war. My girl friends, too, were almost exclusively Nisei. I retreated quite thoroughly into the support and comfort afforded by the Japanese American campus community, and in that separate and segregated world, I felt, at the time, quite content.

Looking back today, our naiveté—my friends' and mine—seems

quite incredible. The world then was a simpler place and we had not developed the sophistication or the social consciousness of more recent college students. Often we were more concerned about the next dance or football game than we were about the world beyond our campus. But I believe this was true of the general college population as well as of the Nisei I knew. Our vision in those days was certainly limited and self-involved. I majored in English, history, and philosophy without a thought as to how I could earn a living after graduation.

My contact with the white world was not totally closed off during my college years, however, for as a family we continued to have several close white friends. Two of my mother's closest friends were, in fact, white women, and her relationships with them, unfettered by the strictures of Japanese etiquette, gave her pleasure in an entirely different way than did her friendships with Issei women.

The Nisei Christian community was another source of social contact for my sister and me. Once a year, a three-day Northern California Young People's Christian Conference was held and attended by hundreds of Nisei from various parts of the state. One or two out-of-town delegates usually stayed with us, and when my sister and I were in college, we became active in the group, sometimes chairing various committees.

If we hadn't had these ethnic organizations to join, I think few Nisei would have had the opportunity to hold positions of leadership or responsibility. At one time I was president of the campus Japanese Women's Student Club, a post I know I would not have held in a non-Japanese campus organization. Similarly, my sister was vice-chairman of the Northern California Christian Conference, but she probably would not have been named to such a post even in a Christian organization unless the group was exclusively Japanese.

Although I went to the university in Berkeley, my sister decided to go to Mills College in Oakland and majored there in child development. On graduating in 1940, however, she could find no work in her field as a certified nursery school teacher. Eventually she found a job as a "governess" to a three-year-old white child in Oakland, but was little more than a nursemaid and was given her meals separately in the kitchen. It wasn't until after the war that she finally found a job as a nursery school teacher in a private school in New York City.

My sister, however, was certainly not alone in facing such bleak employment opportunities. Before World War II, most of the Nisei men who graduated from the university as engineers, pharmacists, accountants, or whatever seldom found employment in their field of study. Many worked as clerks in the tourist gift shops of San Francisco's Chinatown, or as grocery boys, or as assistants in their fathers' businesses. Some turned to gardening, one area in which employers seemed happy to hire Japanese. A few found employment in the Japan-based business firms of San Francisco, but here too they were not fully accepted because they were Japanese Americans and not Japanese nationals.

We Nisei were, in effect, rejected as inferior Americans by our own country and rejected as inferior by the country of our parents as well. We were neither totally American nor totally Japanese, but a unique fusion of the two. Small wonder that many of us felt insecure and ambivalent and retreated into our own special subculture where we were fully accepted.

It was in such a climate, at such a time, in December of 1941 that the Japanese bombs fell on Pearl Harbor.

3. Pearl Harbor

It was one of those rare Sundays when we had no guests for dinner. My parents, sister, and I had just come home from church and were having a quiet lunch when we heard a frenzied voice on the radio break in on the program. The Japanese had attacked Pearl Harbor.

"Oh no," Mama cried out. "It can't be true."

"Of course not," Papa reassured her. "And if it is, it's only the work of a fanatic."

We all agreed with him. Of course it could only be an aberrant act of some crazy irresponsible fool. It never for a moment occurred to any of us that this meant war. As a matter of fact, I was more concerned about my approaching finals at the university than I was with this bizarre news and went to the library to study. When I got there, I found clusters of Nisei students anxiously discussing the shocking event. But we all agreed it was only a freak incident and turned our attention to our books. I stayed at the library until 5:00 P.M. giving no further thought to the attack on Pearl Harbor.

When I got home, the house was filled with an uneasy quiet. A strange man sat in our living room and my father was gone. The FBI had come to pick him up, as they had dozens of other Japanese men. Executives of Japanese business firms, shipping lines, and banks, men active in local Japanese associations, teachers of Japanese language schools, virtually every leader of the Japanese American community along the West Coast had been seized almost immediately.

Actually the FBI had come to our house twice, once in the absence of my parents and sister who, still not realizing the serious nature of the attack, had gone out to visit friends. Their absence, I suppose, had been cause for suspicion and the FBI or police had broken in to search our house without a warrant. On returning, my father, believing that we had been burglarized, immediately called the police. Two policemen appeared promptly with three FBI men and suggested that my father check to see if his valuables were missing. They were, of course, undisturbed, but their location was thereby revealed. Two of the FBI men requested that my father accompany them "for a short while" to be questioned, and my father went willingly. The other FBI man remained with my mother and sister to intercept all phone calls and to inform anyone who called that they were indisposed.

One policeman stationed himself at the front door and the other at the rear. When two of our white friends came to see how we were, they were not permitted to enter or speak to my mother and sister, who, for all practical purposes, were prisoners in our home.

By the time I came home, only one FBI man remained but I was alarmed at the startling turn of events during my absence. In spite of her own anxiety, Mama in her usual thoughtful way was serving tea to the FBI agent. He tried to be friendly and courteous, reassuring me that my father would return safely in due time. But I couldn't share my mother's gracious attitude toward him. Papa was gone, and his abrupt custody into the hands of the FBI seemed an ominous portent of worse things to come. I had no inclination to have tea with one of its agents, and went abruptly to my room, slamming the door shut.

Eventually, after a call from headquarters, the FBI agent left, and Mama, Kay, and I were alone at last. Mama made supper and we sat down to eat, but no one was hungry. Without Papa things just weren't the same, and none of us dared voice the fear that sat like a heavy black stone inside each of us.

"Let's leave the porch light on and the screen door unlatched," Mama said hopefully. "Maybe Papa will be back later tonight."

But the next morning the light was still burning, and we had no idea of his whereabouts. All that day and for three days that followed, we had no knowledge of what had happened to my father. And somehow during those days, I struggled through my finals.

It wasn't until the morning of the fifth day that one of the men apprehended with my father, but released because he was an American citizen, called to tell us that my father was being detained with about one hundred other Japanese men at the Immigration Detention Quarters in San Francisco. The following day a postcard arrived from Papa telling us where he was and asking us to send him his shaving kit and some clean clothes. "Don't worry, I'm all right," he wrote, but all we knew for certain was that he was alive and still in San Francisco.

As soon as permission was granted, we went to visit him at the Immigration Detention Quarters, a drab, dreary institutional structure. We went in, anxious and apprehensive, and were told to wait in a small room while my father was summoned from another part of the building. As I stepped to the door and looked down the dingy hallway, I saw Papa coming toward me with a uniformed guard following close behind. His steps were eager, but he looked worn and tired.

"Papa! Are you all right?"

He hugged each of us.

"I'm all right. I'm fine," he reassured us.

But our joy in seeing him was short-lived, for he told us that he was among a group of ninety men who would be transferred soon to an army internment camp in Missoula, Montana.

"Montana!" we exclaimed. "But we won't be able to see you anymore then."

"I know," Papa said, "but you can write me letters and I'll write you too. Write often, and be very careful—all of you. Kay and Yo, you girls take good care of Mama." His concern was more for us than for himself.

When it was time to say goodbye, none of us could speak for the ache in our hearts. My sister and I began to cry. And it was Mama who was the strong one.

The three of us watched Papa go down the dark hallway with the guard and disappear around a corner. He was gone, and we didn't know if we would ever see him again. There were rumors that men such as my father were to be held as hostages in reprisal for atrocities committed by the Japanese soldiers. If the Japanese killed American prisoners, it was possible my father might be among those killed in reprisal.

It was the first time in our lives that Papa had been separated from us against his will. We returned home in silent gloom, my sister dabbing at her eyes and blowing her nose as she drove us back to Berkeley. When we got home, we comforted ourselves by immediately packing and shipping a carton of warm clothing to Papa in Montana, glad for the opportunity to do something to help him.

As soon as our friends heard that my father had been interned, they gathered around to give us support and comfort, and for several days running we had over fifteen callers a day.

Upon reaching Montana, my father wrote immediately, his major concern being whether we would have enough money for our daily needs. He and my mother were now classified as "enemy aliens" and his bank account had been blocked immediately. For weeks there was total confusion regarding the amount that could be withdrawn from such blocked accounts for living expenses, and early reports indicated it would be only $100 a month.

"Withdraw as much as you can from my account," Papa wrote to us. "I don't want you girls to dip into your own savings accounts unless absolutely necessary."

As the oldest citizen of our household, my sister now had to assume responsibility for managing our business affairs, and it was not an easy task. There were many important papers and documents we needed, but the FBI had confiscated all of my father's keys, including those to his safe deposit box, and their inaccessibility was a problem for us.

We exchanged a flurry of letters as my father tried to send detailed instructions on how to endorse checks on his behalf; how to withdraw money from his accounts; when and how to pay the premiums on his car and life insurance policies; what to do about filing his income tax returns which he could not prepare without his records; and later, when funds were available, how to purchase defense bonds for him. Another time he asked us to send him a check for a fellow internee who needed a loan.

My father had always managed the business affairs of our household, and my mother, sister, and I were totally unprepared to cope with such tasks. Our confusion and bewilderment were overwhelming, and we could sense my father's frustration and anguish at being unable to help us except through censored letters, and later through internee telegrams which were permitted to discourage letter-writing.

Papa's letters were always in English, not only for the benefit of the censor, but for my sister and me. And we could tell from each one that he was carefully reviewing in his mind every aspect of our lives in Berkeley.

"Don't forget to lubricate the car," he would write. "And be sure to prune the roses in January. Brush Laddie every day and give him a pat for me. Don't forget to send a monthly check to Grandma and take my Christmas offering to church."

In every letter he reassured us about his health, sent greetings to his friends, and expressed concern about members of our church.

"Tell those friends at church whose businesses have been closed not to be discouraged," he wrote in one of his first letters. "Tell them things will get better before long."

And he asked often about his garden.

From the early days of my father's detention, there had been talk of a review board that would hold hearings to determine whether and when each man would be released. Although Papa's letters were never discouraging in other respects, he cautioned us not to be optimistic whenever he wrote of the hearings. We all assumed it would be a long, slow process that might require months or even years.

It developed that hearings for each of the interned men were to be conducted by a Board of Review comprised of the district attorney, representatives of the FBI, and immigration authorities of the area in which the men had formerly resided. The recommendation of the review board plus papers and affidavits of support were to be sent to Washington for a final decision by the attorney general. As soon as we learned of this procedure, we asked several of our white friends to send affidavits verifying my father's loyalty to the United States and supporting his early release. They all responded immediately, eager to do anything they could to help him.

The interned men did not dare hope for early release, but they were anxious to have the hearings over with. As they were called in for their interviews, some were photographed full-face only, while others were photographed in profile as well, and it was immediately rumored that those photographed twice would be detained as hostages. Two of the questions they were asked at the interview were, "Which country do you think will win the war?" and "If you had a gun in your hands, at whom would you shoot, the Americans or the Japanese?" In reply to the second question, most answered they would have to shoot straight up.

In accordance with Army policy, the men were never informed of plans in advance and were moved before they became too familiar with one installation. One morning half the men in my father's barrack were summoned, told that they were being shipped to another camp, and stripped of everything but the clothes on their backs. They were then loaded onto buses, with only a few minutes to say goodbye to their friends. Their destination was unknown.

Fortunately, my father was one of those who remained behind. He was also one of those who had been photographed only once, and at the time this seemed to him a faint but hopeful sign of eventual release.

4. Evacuation

⌒₩₩ When the war broke out, my sister was still taking care of the three-year-old child in Oakland. Her employers called immediately to reassure her that they wanted her to continue working for them, but she left to devote full time to her duties as head of our household.

I continued to attend classes at the university hoping to complete the semester, but the Nisei population on campus was dwindling rapidly. Already rumors of a forced mass "evacuation"[1] of the Japanese on the West Coast were circulating, and many Nisei students hurried home to various parts of California to avoid separation from their families. Others returned because they had to take over the businesses and farms abruptly abandoned when their fathers had been seized and interned.

I wasn't aware of any violence against the Japanese in Berkeley, but there were many reports of terrorism in rural communities, and the parents of one of my classmates in Brawley were shot to death by anti-Japanese fanatics.

One evening when some friends and I were having a late snack at a Berkeley restaurant, we were accosted by an angry Filipino man who vividly described what the Japanese soldiers were doing to his home-

1. The term "evacuation" was the Army's official euphemism for our forced removal, just as "non-alien" was used when American citizen was meant. "Assembly center" and "relocation center," terms employed to designate the concentration camps in which we were incarcerated, were also part of the new terminology developed by the United States government and the Army to misrepresent the true nature of their acts. I use them in this book because these were the terms we used at the time.

land. His fists were clenched and his face contorted with rage. Fortunately, he had no weapon, and he left after venting his anger on us verbally, but he had filled us with fear. It was the first time in my life I had been threatened with violence, and it was a terrifying moment.

We were already familiar with social and economic discrimination, but now we learned what it was to be afraid because of our Japanese faces. We tried to go on living as normally as possible, behaving as other American citizens. Most Nisei had never been to Japan. The United States of America was our only country and we were totally loyal to it. Wondering how we could make other Americans understand this, we bought defense bonds, signed up for civilian defense, and cooperated fully with every wartime regulation.

Still the doubts existed. Even one of our close white friends asked, "Did you have any idea the Pearl Harbor attack was coming?" It was a question that stunned and hurt us.

As the weeks passed, rumors of a forced mass evacuation of the Japanese on the West Coast became increasingly persistent. The general public believed the false charges of sabotage in Hawaii, given credence by statements (with no basis in fact) from such government officials as Secretary of the Navy Frank Knox, who told the press he felt the Pearl Harbor attack was the result of espionage and sabotage by Japanese Americans. Rumors of fifth column activity in California were also allowed to circulate freely with no official denial, although they were later completely refuted.

At the time California already had a long history of anti-Asian activity, legitimized by such laws as those that restricted immigration and land ownership. Racists and pressure groups of long standing, whose economic self-interests would be served by the removal of the Japanese, quickly intensified their campaigns of vilification against the Japanese Americans.

They were aided in their shabby efforts by irresponsible and inflammatory statements by the radio and press, which usually referred to the Japanese Americans as "Japs," thus linking us to the enemy in the public mind. They also circulated totally unfounded stories. The Japanese Americans, they reported, had cut arrows in the sugar cane to guide the Japanese bombers to Pearl Harbor; they had interfered with vital United States communications by radio signals; they were treacherous, and loyal only to the Emperor of Japan; they had used their fishing boats to conduct espionage. So completely were these falsehoods accepted by the public that I have heard some of them repeated even today by those who still believe the forced removal of the Japanese Americans was justified.

Compounding the mounting hatred, fear, and suspicion of the Japanese Americans on the West Coast were cynical manipulations of public opinion at many high levels of the government and the military. Earl Warren, then attorney general of California, testified that Japanese Americans had "infiltrated . . . every strategic spot" in California. He further made the appalling statement that there was no way to determine loyalty when dealing with people of Japanese ancestry, as opposed to those who were white.

On the floor of the House of Representatives, Congressman John Rankin urged, "I'm for catching every Japanese in America, Alaska and Hawaii now and putting them in concentration camps . . . Damn them! Let's get rid of them now!"

We now know that in the fall of 1941, President Franklin D. Roosevelt and his secretaries of state, war, and the navy had read the report of Curtis B. Munson (special representative of the State Department) written after he had made an intensive survey of the Japanese Americans in Hawaii and on the West Coast. In this report Munson stated that he found "a remarkable, even extraordinary degree of loyalty" among the Japanese Americans. Although this corroborated previous government findings, and although no evidence of disloyalty or sabotage on the part of Japanese Americans could be found, our government leaders were not persuaded. Overriding the concerns voiced by the attorney general and the justice department, they made the decision to forcibly evict all West Coast Japanese—"aliens and non-aliens"—under the guise of "military necessity." Furthermore, this decision was sanctioned by the Supreme Court of the land.

The fact that there was no mass eviction in Hawaii, which was closer to Japan and where the Japanese Americans constituted a third of the population, clearly invalidated the government's claim that the evacuation was a military necessity.

The confluence of all these factors, coupled with the fear and hys-

In 1942, hatred against the Japanese Americans was fueled by newspapers that usually referred to us as "Japs." *Courtesy of National Archives*

teria exacerbated by severe United States losses in the Pacific war, eventually combined to make the evacuation a tragic reality for us.

By the end of February my father's letters and telegrams began to reflect his growing concern over the matter as well. "Worrying about reported mass evacuation," he wired. "Please telegraph actual situation there."

But we didn't know what the actual situation was. None of us could believe such an unthinkable event would actually take place. Gradually, however, we began to prepare for its possibility. One night a friend came to see us as we were packing our books in a large wood crate.

"What on earth are you doing?" he asked incredulously. "There won't be any evacuation. How could the United States government intern its own citizens? It would be unconstitutional."

But only a few weeks later, we were to discover how wrong he was.

By February 1942, there was no longer any doubt as to the government's intention. On the nineteenth of that month, President Roosevelt issued Executive Order 9066, authorizing the secretary of war and his military commanders to prescribe areas from which "any or all persons may be excluded." Although use of the word "Japanese" was avoided in this order, it was directed solely at people of Japanese ancestry. The fact that there was no mass removal of persons of German or Italian descent, even though our country was also at war with Germany and Italy, affirmed the racial bias of this directive.

By the middle of March, Lieutenant General John L. DeWitt began to execute the order and set in motion the removal from Military Area Number One, along the entire West Coast, of over 120,000 men, women, and children of Japanese ancestry, the majority of whom were American citizens.[2] From his later testimony at a House Naval Affairs Sub-committee on Housing (April 13, 1943), it is apparent that he performed this task with undisguised enthusiasm. He is quoted as having said, "It makes no difference whether the Japanese is theoretically

2. Of these, some 10,000 made their own way outside the excluded zones, while the remaining 110,000 were incarcerated.

a citizen. He is still a Japanese. Giving him a scrap of paper won't change him. I don't care what they do with the Japs so long as they don't send them back here. A Jap is a Jap."

With such a man heading the Western Defense Command, it is not surprising that no time was lost in carrying out the evacuation order.

Both the Fifth and Fourteenth Amendments to the Constitution providing for "due process of law" and "equal protection under the law for all citizens," were flagrantly ignored in the name of military expediency, and the forced eviction was carried out purely on the basis of race.

Stunned by this unprecedented act of our government, we Nisei were faced with the anguishing dilemma of contesting our government's orders and risking imprisonment (as a few courageous Nisei did) or of complying with the government edict.

Because the FBI had interned most of the Issei leaders of the community, effectively decimating Issei organizations, the vacuum in leadership was filled by the Japanese American Citizens League, then led by a group of relatively young Nisei. The JACL met in emergency session attempting to arrive at the best possible solution to an intolerable situation. Perceiving that a compromise with the government was impossible, and rejecting a strategy of total opposition, because it might lead to violence and bloodshed, the JACL leaders decided the only choice was to cooperate "under protest" with the government.

My sister and I were angry that our country could deprive us of our civil rights in so cavalier a manner, but we had been raised to respect and to trust those in authority. To us resistance or confrontation, such as we know them today, was unthinkable and of course would have had no support from the American public. We naively believed at the time that cooperating with the government edict was the best way to help our country.

The first mass removal of the Japanese began in Terminal Island, a fishing community near San Pedro, and because these people were close to a naval base, their treatment was harsh. With most of their men already interned as my father was, the remaining families had to cope with a three-day deadline to get out of their homes. In frantic haste they were forced to sell their houses, businesses, and property. Many were exploited cruelly and suffered great financial losses.

We knew it was simply a matter of time before we would be notified to evacuate Berkeley as well. A five-mile travel limit and an 8:00 P.M. curfew had already been imposed on all Japanese Americans since March, and enemy aliens were required to register and obtain identification cards. Radios with short wave, cameras, binoculars, and firearms were designated as "contraband" and had to be turned in to the police. Obediently adhering to all regulations, we even brought our box cameras to the Berkeley police station where they remained for the duration of the war.

We were told by the military that "voluntary evacuation" to areas outside the West Coast restricted zone could be made before the final notice for each sector was issued. The move was hardly "voluntary" as the Army labeled it, and most Japanese had neither the funds to leave nor a feasible destination. The three of us also considered leaving "voluntarily," but like the others, we had no one to go to outside the restricted zone.

Some of our friends warned us to consider what life would be like for three women in a "government assembly center" and urged us to go anywhere in order to remain free. On the other hand, there were those who told us of the arrests, violence, and vigilantism encountered by some who had fled "voluntarily." Either decision would have been easier had my father been with us, but without him both seemed fraught with uncertainties.

In Montana my father, too, was worried about our safety. He wrote us of an incident in Sacramento where men had gained entrance to a Japanese home by posing as FBI agents and then attacked the mother and daughter. "Please be very careful," he urged. We decided, finally, to go to the government camp where we would be with friends and presumably safe from violence. We also hoped my father's release might be facilitated if he could join us under government custody.

Each day we watched the papers for the evacuation orders covering the Berkeley area. On April 21, the headlines read: "Japs Given Evacuation Orders Here." I felt numb as I read the front page story. "Moving swiftly, without any advance notice, the Western Defense Command today ordered Berkeley's estimated 1,319 Japanese, aliens and citizens alike, evacuated to the Tanforan Assembly Center by noon, May 1." (This gave us exactly ten days' notice.) "Evacuees will report at the Civil Control Station being set up in Pilgrim Hall of the First Congregational Church . . . between the hours of 8:00 A.M. and 5:00 P.M. next Saturday and Sunday."

This was Exclusion Order Number Nineteen, which was to uproot us from our homes and send us into the Tanforan Assembly Center in San Bruno, a hastily converted racetrack.

All Japanese were required to register before the departure date, and my sister, as head of the family, went to register for us. She came home with baggage and name tags that were to bear our family number and be attached to all our belongings. From that day on we became Family Number 13453.

Although we had been preparing for the evacuation orders, still when they were actually issued, it was a sickening shock.

"Ten days! We have only ten days to get ready!" my sister said frantically. Each day she rushed about, not only taking care of our business affairs, but, as our only driver, searching for old crates and cartons for packing, and taking my mother on various errands as well.

Mama still couldn't seem to believe that we would have to leave. "How can we clear out in ten days a house we've lived in for fifteen years?" she asked sadly.

But my sister and I had no answers for her.

Mama had always been a saver, and she had a tremendous accumulation of possessions. Her frugal upbringing had caused her to save string, wrapping paper, bags, jars, boxes, even bits of silk thread left over from sewing, which were tied end to end and rolled up into a silk ball. Tucked away in the corners of her desk and bureau drawers were such things as small stuffed animals, wooden toys, kokeshi dolls, marbles, and even a half-finished pair of socks she was knitting for a teddy bear's paw. Many of these were "found objects" that the child in her couldn't bear to discard, but they often proved useful in providing diversion for some fidgety visiting child. These were the simple things to dispose of.

More difficult were the boxes that contained old letters from her family and friends, our old report cards from the first grade on, dozens of albums of family photographs, notebooks and sketch pads full of our childish drawings, valentines and Christmas cards we had made for our parents, innumerable guest books filled with the signatures and friendly words of those who had once been entertained. These were the things my mother couldn't bear to throw away. Because we didn't own our house, we could leave nothing behind. We had to clear the house completely, and everything in it had either to be packed for storage or thrown out.

We surveyed with desperation the vast array of dishes, lacquerware, silverware, pots and pans, books, paintings, porcelain and pottery, furniture, linens, rugs, records, curtains, garden tools, cleaning equipment, and clothing that filled our house. We put up a sign in our window reading, "Living room sofa and chair for sale." We sold things we should have kept and packed away foolish trifles we should have discarded. We sold our refrigerator, our dining room set, two sofas, an easy chair, and a brand new vacuum cleaner with attachments. Without a sensible scheme in our heads, and lacking the practical judgment of my father, the three of us packed frantically and sold recklessly. Although the young people of our church did what they could to help us, we felt desperate as the deadline approached. Our only thought was to get the house emptied in time, for we knew the Army would not wait.

Organizations such as the First Congregational Church of Berkeley were extremely helpful in anticipating the needs of the panic-stricken Japanese and provided immediate, practical assistance. Families of the church offered storage space to those who needed it, and we took several pieces of furniture to be stored in the basement of one such home. Another non-Japanese friend offered to take our books and stored more than eight large cartons for us. In typical Japanese fashion, my mother took gifts to express her gratitude to each person who helped us.

Our two neighboring families, one Swiss and the other Norwegian, were equally helpful. We had grown up with the two blond Norwegian girls, whose ages nearly matched my sister's and mine. We had played everything from "house" to "cops and robbers" with them and had spent many hot summer afternoons happily sipping their father's home-made root beer with them.

The two boys in the Swiss family were younger, and I had taken one of them to grammar school every day when he was in kindergarten. In loving admiration, he had offered to marry me when he grew up. We were close to our neighbors and they both extended the warmth of their friendship to us in those hectic days. We left our piano and a few pieces of furniture with one, and we piled all the miscellaneous objects that remained on the last day into the garage of the other.

The objects too large to leave with friends, such as beds, mattresses and springs, extra quilts, and rugs, we stored in a commercial storage house, whose monthly statements never failed to reach us even in the stalls of Tanforan or, later, in the sandy wastes of Utah.

Not knowing what crude inadequate communal facilities we might have in camp, we also took the precaution of getting typhoid shots and lost a day of packing, which we could ill afford, as we nursed sore arms and aching heads.

Two problems that remained unsolved until very near our departure deadline were what to do with Laddie, our pet collie, and our almost new Buick sedan. A business associate of my father's offered to store the car in his garage for us, but a few months after we entered Tanforan he needed the space and sold it for us for $600.

Our pedigreed Scotch collie was a gentle friendly dog, but our friends didn't want to take him because of his age. In desperation, I sent a letter to our university's student newspaper, the *Daily Californian*.

I am one of the Japanese American students soon to be evacuated and have a male Scotch collie that can't come with me. Can anyone give him a home? If interested, please call me immediately at Berkeley 7646W.

I was quickly deluged with calls, one of which was from a fraternity that wanted a mascot. But we decided on the first boy who called because he seemed kind and genuinely concerned.

"I'll pay you for him," he offered, trying to be helpful.

But how could we accept money for our old family pet? We eventually gave the boy everything that belonged to Laddie, including his doghouse, leash, food bowl, and brushes.

It was a particularly sad day for my sister, who was the avid animal-lover of our family. It was she who had begged, cajoled, and coerced my parents into getting all of our dogs. But once they became our pets, we all loved them, and Mama used to cook a separate pot of vegetables to feed our dogs along with their cans of Dr. Ross's dog food.

Although the new owner of our pet had promised faithfully to write us in camp, we never heard from him. When, finally, we had a friend investigate for us, we learned that the boy hadn't the heart to write us that Laddie had died only a few weeks after we left Berkeley.

By now I had to leave the university, as did all the other Nisei students. We had stayed as long as we could to get credit for the spring semester, which was crucial for those of us who were seniors. My professors gave me a final grade on the basis of my midterm grades and the university granted all Nisei indefinite leaves of absence.

During the last few weeks on campus, my friends and I became sentimental and took pictures of each other at favorite campus sites. The war had jolted us into a crisis whose impact was too enormous for us to fully comprehend, and we needed these small remembrances of happier times to take with us as we went our separate ways to various government camps throughout California.

The *Daily Californian* published another letter from a Nisei student that read in part:

> We are no longer to see the campus to which many of us have been so attached for the past four years. . . . It is hoped that others who are leaving will not cherish feelings of bitterness. True, we are being uprooted from the lives that we have always lived, but if the security of the nation rests upon our leaving, then we will gladly do our part. We have come through a period of hysteria, but we cannot blame the American public for the vituperations of a small but vociferous minority of self-seeking politicians and special interest groups. We cannot condemn democracy because a few have misused the mechanism of democracy to gain their own ends. . . . In the hard days ahead, we shall try to re-create the spirit which has made us so reluctant to leave now, and our wish to those who remain is that they maintain here the democratic ideals that have operated in the past. We hope to come back and find them here.

These were brave idealistic words, but I believe they reflected the feelings of most of us at that time.

As our packing progressed, our house grew increasingly barren and our garden took on a shabby look that would have saddened my father. My mother couldn't bear to leave her favorite plants to strangers and dug up her special rose, London Smoke carnations, and yellow calla lilies to take to a friend for safekeeping.

One day a neighboring woman rang our bell and asked for one of Papa's prize gladiolas that she had fancied as she passed by. It seemed a heartless, avaricious gesture, and I was indignant, just as I was when people told me the evacuation was for our own protection. My mother, however, simply handed the woman a shovel and told her to help herself. "Let her have it," she said, "if it will make her happy."

Gradually ugly gaps appeared in the garden that had once been my parents' delight and, like our house, it began to take on an empty abandoned look.

Toward the end, my mother sat Japanese fashion, her legs folded beneath her, in the middle of her vacant bedroom sorting out the contents of many dusty boxes that had been stored on her closet shelves.

She was trying to discard some of the poems she had scribbled on scraps of paper, clippings she had saved, notebooks of her writings, and bundles of old letters from her family and friends. Only now have I come to realize what a heartbreaking task this must have been for her as her native land confronted in war the land of her children. She knew she would be cut off from her mother, brothers, and sister until that war ended. She knew she could neither hear from them nor write to tell them of her concern and love. The letters she had kept for so long were her last link with them for the time being and she couldn't bear to throw them out. She put most of them in her trunk where they remained, not only during the war, but until her death. In the end, it fell to me to burn them in our backyard, and I watched the smoke drift up into the sky, perhaps somewhere to reach the spirit of my gentle mother.

Our bedrooms were now barren except for three old mattresses on which we slept until the day we left. But in one corner of my mother's room there was an enormous shapeless canvas blanket bag which we called our "camp bundle." Into its flexible and obliging depths we tossed anything that wouldn't fit into the two suitcases we each planned to take. We had been instructed to take only what we could carry, so from time to time we would have a practice run, trying to see if we could walk while carrying two full suitcases.

Having given us these directions, the Army with its own peculiar logic also instructed us to bring our bedding, dishes, and eating utensils. Obviously the only place for these bulky items was in the "camp bundle." Into it we packed our blankets, pillows, towels, rubber boots, a tea kettle, a hot plate, dishes and silverware, umbrellas, and anything else that wouldn't fit in our suitcases. As May 1 drew near, it grew to gigantic and cumbersome proportions, and by no stretch of our imagination could we picture ourselves staggering into camp with it.

"Mama, what'll we ever do with that enormous thing?" my sister worried.

"We obviously can't carry that thing on our backs," I observed.

But all Mama could say was, "I'm sure things will work out somehow."

There was nothing to be done but to go on filling it and hope for the best. In the meantime, we watched uneasily as it continued to grow, bulging in all directions like some wild living thing.

We could have been spared our anxiety and agonizing had we known trucks would be available to transport our baggage to camp. But it is entirely possible the omission of this information in our instructions was intentional to discourage us from taking too much baggage with us.

The night before we left, our Swiss neighbors invited us to dinner. It was a fine feast served with our neighbors' best linens, china, and silverware. With touching concern they did their best to make our last evening in Berkeley as pleasant as possible.

I sat on the piano bench that had been in our home until a few days before and thought of the times I had sat on it when we entertained our many guests. Now, because of the alarming succession of events that even then seemed unreal, I had become a guest myself in our neighbors' home.

When we returned to our dark empty house, our Norwegian neighbors came to say goodbye. The two girls brought gifts for each of us and hugged us goodbye.

"Come back soon," they said as they left.

But none of us knew when we would ever be back. We lay down on our mattresses and tried to sleep, knowing it was our last night in our house on Stuart Street.

Neat and conscientious to the end, my mother wanted to leave our house in perfect condition. That last morning she swept the entire place, her footsteps echoing sadly throughout the vacant house. Our Swiss neighbors brought us a cheering breakfast on bright-colored

Baggage was a major problem, for we were told to take into camp only what we could carry. *Courtesy of National Archives*

From the moment we boarded the buses for Tanforan, every move we made was under armed guard. *Courtesy of National Archives*

dishes and then drove us to the First Congregational Church designated as the Civil Control Station where we were to report.

We were too tense and exhausted to fully sense the terrible wrench of leaving our home, and when we arrived at the church, we said our goodbyes quickly. I didn't even turn back to wave, for we were quickly absorbed into the large crowd of Japanese that had already gathered on the church grounds.

It wasn't until I saw the armed guards standing at each doorway, their bayonets mounted and ready, that I realized the full horror of the situation. Then my knees sagged, my stomach began to churn, and I very nearly lost my breakfast.

Hundreds of Japanese Americans were crowded into the great hall of the church and the sound of their voices pressed close around me. Old people sat quietly, waiting with patience and resignation for whatever was to come. Mothers tried to comfort crying infants, young children ran about the room, and some teenagers tried to put up a brave front by making a social opportunity of the occasion. The women of the church were serving tea and sandwiches, but very few of us had any inclination to eat.

Before long, we were told to board the buses that lined the street outside, and the people living nearby came out of their houses to watch the beginning of our strange migration. Most of them probably watched with curious and morbid fascination, some perhaps even with a little sadness. But many may have been relieved and glad to see us go.

Mama, Kay, and I climbed onto one of the buses and it began its one-way journey down familiar streets we had traveled so often in our own car. We crossed the Bay Bridge, went on beyond San Francisco, and sped down the Bayshore Highway. Some of the people on the bus talked nervously, one or two wept, but most sat quietly, keeping their thoughts to themselves and their eyes on the window, as familiar landmarks slipped away one by one.

As we rode down the highway, the grandstand of the Tanforan racetrack gradually came into view, and I could see a high barbed wire fence surrounding the entire area, pierced at regular intervals by tall guard towers. This was to be our temporary home until the government could construct inland camps far removed from the West Coast.

The bus made a sharp turn and swung slowly into the racetrack grounds. As I looked out the window for a better view, I saw armed guards close and bar the barbed wire gates behind us. We were in the Tanforan Assembly Center now and there was no turning back.

5. *Tanforan: A Horse Stall for Four*

 As the bus pulled up to the grandstand, I could see hundreds of Japanese Americans jammed along the fence that lined the track. These people had arrived a few days earlier and were now watching for the arrival of friends or had come to while away the empty hours that had suddenly been thrust upon them.

As soon as we got off the bus, we were directed to an area beneath the grandstand where we registered and filled out a series of forms. Our baggage was inspected for contraband, a cursory medical check was made, and our living quarters assigned. We were to be housed in Barrack 16, Apartment 40. Fortunately, some friends who had arrived earlier found us and offered to help us locate our quarters.

It had rained the day before and the hundreds of people who had trampled on the track had turned it into a miserable mass of slippery mud. We made our way on it carefully, helping my mother who was dressed just as she would have been to go to church. She wore a hat, gloves, her good coat, and her Sunday shoes, because she would not have thought of venturing outside our house dressed in any other way.

Everywhere there were black tar-papered barracks that had been hastily erected to house the 8,000 Japanese Americans of the area who had been uprooted from their homes. Barrack 16, however, was not among them, and we couldn't find it until we had traveled half the length of the track and gone beyond it to the northern rim of the race-track compound.

Finally one of our friends called out, "There it is, beyond that row of eucalyptus trees." Barrack 16 was not a barrack at all, but a long stable raised a few feet off the ground with a broad ramp the horses had used to reach their stalls. Each stall was now numbered and ours was number 40. That the stalls should have been called "apartments" was a euphemism so ludicrous it was comical.

When we reached stall number 40, we pushed open the narrow door and looked uneasily into the vacant darkness. The stall was about ten by twenty feet and empty except for three folded Army cots lying on the floor. Dust, dirt, and wood shavings covered the linoleum that had been laid over manure-covered boards, the smell of horses hung in the air, and the whitened corpses of many insects still clung to the hastily white-washed walls.

High on either side of the entrance were two small windows which were our only source of daylight. The stall was divided into two sections by Dutch doors worn down by teeth marks, and each stall in the stable was separated from the adjoining one only by rough partitions that stopped a foot short of the sloping roof. That space, while perhaps a good source of ventilation for the horses, deprived us of all but visual privacy, and we couldn't even be sure of that because of the crevices and knotholes in the dividing walls.

Because our friends had already spent a day as residents of Tanforan, they had become adept at scrounging for necessities. One found a broom and swept the floor for us. Two of the boys went to the barracks where mattresses were being issued, stuffed the ticking with straw themselves, and came back with three for our cots.

Nothing in the camp was ready. Everything was only half-finished. I wondered how much the nation's security would have been threatened had the Army permitted us to remain in our homes a few more days until the camps were adequately prepared for occupancy by families.

By the time we had cleaned out the stall and set up the cots, it was time for supper. Somehow, in all the confusion, we had not had lunch, so I was eager to get to the main mess hall which was located beneath the grandstand.

The sun was going down as we started along the muddy track, and a cold piercing wind swept in from the bay. When we arrived, there were six long weaving lines of people waiting to get into the mess hall. We took our place at the end of one of them, each of us clutching a plate and silverware borrowed from friends who had already received their baggage.

Shivering in the cold, we pressed close together trying to shield Mama from the wind. As we stood in what seemed a breadline for the destitute, I felt degraded, humiliated, and overwhelmed with a longing for home. And I saw the unutterable sadness on my mother's face.

This was only the first of many lines we were to endure, and we soon discovered that waiting in line was as inevitable a part of Tanforan as the north wind that swept in from the bay stirring up all the dust and litter of the camp.

Once we got inside the gloomy cavernous mess hall, I saw hundreds of people eating at wooden picnic tables, while those who had already eaten were shuffling aimlessly over the wet cement floor. When I reached the serving table and held out my plate, a cook reached into a dishpan full of canned sausages and dropped two onto my plate with his fingers. Another man gave me a boiled potato and a piece of butterless bread.

With 5,000 people to be fed, there were few unoccupied tables, so we separated from our friends and shared a table with an elderly man and a young family with two crying babies. No one at the table spoke to us, and even Mama could seem to find no friendly word to offer as she normally would have done. We tried to eat, but the food wouldn't go down.

"Let's get out of here," my sister suggested.

We decided it would be better to go back to our barrack than to linger in the depressing confusion of the mess hall. It had grown dark by now and since Tanforan had no lights for nighttime occupancy, we had to pick our way carefully down the slippery track.

Once back in our stall, we found it no less depressing, for there was only a single electric light bulb dangling from the ceiling, and a one-inch crevice at the top of the north wall admitted a steady draft of the cold night air. We sat huddled on our cots, bundled in our coats, too cold and miserable even to talk. My sister and I worried about Mama, for she wasn't strong and had recently been troubled with neuralgia which could easily be aggravated by the cold. She in turn was worrying about us, and of course we all worried and wondered about Papa.

Suddenly we heard the sound of a truck stopping outside.

"Hey, Uchida! Apartment 40!" a boy shouted.

I rushed to the door and found the baggage boys trying to heave our enormous "camp bundle" over the railing that fronted our stall.

"What ya got in here anyway?" they shouted good-naturedly as they struggled with the unwieldy bundle. "It's the biggest thing we got on our truck!"

I grinned, embarrassed, but I could hardly wait to get out our belongings. My sister and I fumbled to undo all the knots we had tied into the rope around our bundle that morning and eagerly pulled out the familiar objects from home.

We unpacked our blankets, pillows, sheets, tea kettle, and most welcome of all, our electric hot plate. I ran to the nearest washroom to fill the kettle with water, while Mama and Kay made up the Army cots with our bedding. Once we hooked up the hot plate and put the kettle on to boil, we felt better. We sat close to its warmth, holding our hands toward it as though it were our fireplace at home.

Before long some friends came by to see us, bringing with them the only gift they had—a box of dried prunes. Even the day before, we wouldn't have given the prunes a second glance, but now they were as welcome as the boxes of Maskey's chocolates my father used to bring home from San Francisco.

Mama managed to make some tea for our friends, and we sat around our steaming kettle, munching gratefully on our prunes. We spent most of the evening talking about food and the lack of it, a concern that grew obsessive over the next few weeks when we were constantly hungry.

Our stable consisted of twenty-five stalls facing north which were back to back with an equal number facing south, so we were surrounded on three sides. Living in our stable were an assortment of people—mostly small family units—that included an artist, my father's barber and his wife, a dentist and his wife, an elderly retired couple, a group of Kibei bachelors (Japanese born in the United States but educated in Japan), an insurance salesman and his wife, and a widow with two daughters. To say that we all became intimately acquainted

Our family of four lived in a single horse stall in an old stable at the Tanforan racetrack. *Courtesy of National Archives*

Long lines of internees, clutching their own plates and eating utensils, formed outside the Tanforan mess halls for each meal. *Courtesy of National Archives*

would be an understatement. It was, in fact, communal living, with semi-private cubicles provided only for sleeping.

Our neighbors on one side spent much of their time playing cards, and at all hours of the day we could hear the sound of cards being shuffled and money changing hands. Our other neighbors had a teenage son who spent most of the day with his friends, coming home to his stall at night only after his parents were asleep. Family life began to show signs of strain almost immediately, not only in the next stall but throughout the entire camp.

One Sunday our neighbor's son fell asleep in the rear of his stall with the door bolted from inside. When his parents came home from church, no amount of shouting or banging on the door could awaken the boy.

"Our stupid son has locked us out," they explained, coming to us for help.

I climbed up on my cot and considered pouring water on him over the partition, for I knew he slept just on the other side of it. Instead I dangled a broom over the partition and poked and prodded with it, shouting, "Wake up! Wake up!" until the boy finally bestirred himself and let his parents in. We became good friends with our neighbors after that.

About one hundred feet from our stable were two latrines and two washrooms for our section of camp, one each for men and women. The latrines were crude wooden structures containing eight toilets, separated by partitions, but having no doors. The washrooms were divided into two sections. In the front section was a long tin trough spaced with spigots of hot and cold water where we washed our faces and brushed our teeth. To the rear were eight showers, also separated by partitions, but lacking doors or curtains. The showers were difficult to adjust and we either got scalded by torrents of hot water or shocked by an icy blast of cold. Most of the Issei were unaccustomed to showers, having known the luxury of soaking in deep pine-scented tubs during their years in Japan, and found the showers virtually impossible to use.

Our card-playing neighbor scoured the camp for a container that might serve as a tub, and eventually found a large wooden barrel. She rolled it to the showers, filled it with warm water, and then climbed in for a pleasant and leisurely soak. The greatest compliment she could offer anyone was the use of her private tub.

The lack of privacy in the latrines and showers was an embarrassing hardship especially for the older women, and many would take newspapers to hold over their faces or squares of cloth to tack up for their own private curtain. The Army, obviously ill-equipped to build living quarters for women and children, had made no attempt to introduce even the most common of life's civilities into these camps for us.

During the first few weeks of camp life everything was erratic and in short supply. Hot water appeared only sporadically, and the minute it was available, everyone ran for the showers or the laundry. We had to be clever and quick just to keep clean, and my sister and I often walked a mile to the other end of camp where hot water was in better supply, in order to boost our morale with a hot shower.

Even toilet paper was at a premium, for new rolls would disappear as soon as they were placed in the latrines. The shock of the evacuation compounded by the short supply of every necessity brought out the baser instincts of the internees, and there was little inclination for anyone to feel responsible for anyone else. In the early days, at least, it was everyone for himself or herself.

One morning I saw some women emptying bed pans into the troughs where we washed our faces. The sight was enough to turn my stomach, and my mother quickly made several large signs in Japanese cautioning people against such unsanitary practices. We posted them in conspicuous spots in the washroom and hoped for the best.

Across from the latrines was a double barrack, one containing laundry tubs and the other equipped with clotheslines and ironing boards. Because there were so many families with young children, the laundry tubs were in constant use. The hot water was often gone by 9:00 A.M. and many women got up at 3:00 and 4:00 in the morning to do their wash, all of which, including sheets, had to be done entirely by hand.

We found it difficult to get to the laundry before 9:00 A.M., and by then every tub was taken and there were long lines of people with bags of dirty laundry waiting behind each one. When we finally got to a tub, there was no more hot water. Then we would leave my mother to hold the tub while my sister and I rushed to the washroom where there was a better supply and carried back bucketfuls of hot water as everyone else learned to do. By the time we had finally hung our laundry on lines outside our stall, we were too exhausted to do much else for the rest of the day.

For four days after our arrival we continued to go to the main mess hall for all our meals. My sister and I usually missed breakfast because we were assigned to the early shift and we simply couldn't get there by 7:00 A.M. Dinner was at 4:45 P.M., which was a terrible hour, but not a major problem, as we were always hungry. Meals were uniformly bad and skimpy, with an abundance of starches such as beans and bread. I wrote to my non-Japanese friends in Berkeley shamelessly asking them to send us food, and they obliged with large cartons of cookies, nuts, dried fruit, and jams.

We looked forward with much anticipation to the opening of a half dozen smaller mess halls located throughout the camp. But when ours finally opened, we discovered that the preparation of smaller quantities had absolutely no effect on the quality of the food. We went eagerly to our new mess hall only to be confronted at our first meal with chili con carne, corn, and butterless bread. To assuage our disappointment, a friend and I went to the main mess hall which was still in operation, to see if it had anything better. Much to our amazement and delight, we found small lettuce salads, the first fresh vegetables we had seen in many days. We ate ravenously and exercised enormous self-control not to go back for second and third helpings.

The food improved gradually, and by the time we left Tanforan five months later, we had fried chicken and ice cream for Sunday dinner. By July tubs of soapy water were installed at the mess hall exits so we could wash our plates and utensils on the way out. Being slow eaters, however, we usually found the dishwater tepid and dirty by the time we reached the tubs, and we often rewashed our dishes in the washroom.

Most internees got into the habit of rushing for everything. They ran to the mess halls to be first in line, they dashed inside for the best tables and then rushed through their meals to get to the washtubs before the suds ran out. The three of us, however, seemed to be at the end of every line that formed and somehow never managed to be first for anything.

One of the first things we all did at Tanforan was to make our living quarters as comfortable as possible. A pile of scrap lumber in one corner of camp melted away like snow on a hot day as residents salvaged whatever they could to make shelves and crude pieces of furniture to supplement the Army cots. They also made ingenious containers for carrying their dishes to the mess halls, with handles and lids that grew more and more elaborate in a sort of unspoken competition.

Because of my father's absence, our friends helped us in camp, just as they had in Berkeley, and we relied on them to put up shelves and build a crude table and two benches for us. We put our new camp furniture in the front half of our stall, which was our "living room," and put our three cots in the dark windowless rear section, which we promptly dubbed "the dungeon." We ordered some print fabric by mail and sewed curtains by hand to hang at our windows and to cover our shelves. Each new addition to our stall made it seem a little more like home.

One afternoon about a week after we had arrived at Tanforan, a messenger from the administration building appeared with a telegram for us. It was from my father telling us he had been released on parole from Montana and would be able to join us soon in camp. Papa was coming home. The wonderful news had come like an unexpected gift, but even as we hugged each other in joy, we didn't quite dare believe it until we actually saw him.

The fact that my father had retired from Mitsui two years before the war at the mandatory retirement age of fifty-five (many Japanese firms required early retirement to make room for their younger employees), his record of public and community service, and the affidavits from his friends were probably factors that secured his early release. As a parolee, he would have to account for every move he made until the end of the war and would not be able to leave government custody without a sponsor to vouch for him. But these restrictions didn't seem important at the time. The main thing was that he was coming home.

We had no idea when he would actually return, but the next day another messenger appeared to tell us that my father had already arrived and was waiting for us at the administration building.

My sister and I couldn't wait for Mama, and we ran ahead down the track to the grandstand. We rushed into the waiting room and saw my father waiting for us, looking thinner, but none the worse for wear.

"Papa!" we screamed, and rushed into his arms.

He had returned with two other men, and their families joined us in a grand and tearful reunion. We all had supper together at the main mess hall, and by the time we returned to our stall, word had spread that my father was home. Almost all of our many friends in camp stopped by that evening to welcome him home. It was pure joy and pandemonium as friends crowded into our tiny stall.

My father, a lively conversationalist as always, was brimming with stories of his five-month internment, and as our friends listened eagerly, the light burned in our stall long after the adjoining stalls had grown quiet and dark. From their own stalls our neighbors were listening, and one of them came the next day to tell us how much she had enjoyed my father's descriptions of life in Montana. She often listened to conversations that took place in our stall, sometimes coming later to ask about a point she had missed, or hurrying out from her stall when our friends left to see the face of a voice that had aroused her curiosity.

The night of my father's return was the first of many evenings spent in conversation with our friends as a reunited family. We may have been in a racetrack "assembly center" with four cots now crowded into a stall that had housed a single horse, but we were together once more, and that was something to be grateful for.

In the days following my father's return, we gradually heard more of what had happened to him after we left him at the Immigration Detention Quarters the day of our last visit. He and the other men transferred to Missoula had boarded buses for Oakland and then entrained for Montana. As the train moved northward, cars from Portland and Seattle were added to those from Los Angeles and Oakland, and my father later found many old friends in each contingent. The oldest man in the group was eighty-two.

It was a long forty-eight-hour ride on stiff straight-backed seats, with the blinds drawn day and night and armed guards at each exit. The men had been designated "dangerous enemy aliens" and every precaution was taken against their escape. They had been stripped of all their possessions, including handkerchiefs, and most of them traveled in the clothing they were wearing when so abruptly taken into custody. Some of the men had been apprehended on golf courses, others as they worked in their fields or as they came off their fishing boats. One man who had just undergone surgery for cancer of the stomach four days earlier had been taken directly from his hospital bed. During the course of the journey another man suffered a breakdown and his friends had to force a pencil between his teeth to keep him from biting his tongue.

Once they arrived in Missoula, the men were housed thirty to a barrack, with cots lining both sides of the room, Army fashion. Here all the men, whatever their station in life, were treated alike as prisoners of war. Each was required to take his turn cleaning the barracks and latrines and working in the kitchen as waiter, cook, or dishwasher. My father, who had often helped my mother with some of her household chores, slipped easily into these new roles, rather enjoying the challenge they presented, but other men, who were more traditional Japanese husbands, found it difficult to perform what seemed to them demeaning tasks.

The men were encouraged to become self-governing, and shortly after their arrival, elected a mayor and various committee chairmen. It was typical of my father that he should be elected chairman of the welfare committee since he had had so much experience caring for the sick, the aged, and those in need. He made arrangements for meetings and speakers, and one of his first acts was to establish a church. He also organized and personally attended classes in English composition, grammar, American history, law, and even ballroom dancing, all of which were held daily and taught by internees versed in these subjects. In one of his letters he wrote, "You will be surprised to find me a good dancer when I come home!"

It was also his task to arrange funeral services for the men who died in Montana. The first was a seventy-four-year-old man who died of pneumonia. The second was the man who had been removed from the hospital following surgery. Because the remains of those who died were shipped home directly from the morgue, the interned men were permitted only to hold memorial services for them. Although many of the internees were strangers to each other, the deaths drew them all closer.

Out of the meager funds they were permitted to keep, they contributed generously to purchase flowers and candles for the services, sending the surplus to the families of the men who had died. Just as he often did at our church at home, my father sang a hymn at each of the services as his own special tribute.

All the internees' incoming and outgoing letters were subject to censorship, and many of my father's letters arrived well-ventilated with the holes left by the censor's scissors. Outgoing mail was restricted to three letters a week and my father, a great letter writer, was one of the first to be reprimanded. "I've been warned," he wrote us, "that I write too much and too long." He soon located an old typewriter which he borrowed for his letter-writing to make life easier for the censors, and later had to limit his communications to brief telegrams which included such messages as, "Please give Kay freesia bouquet and hearty greetings on her birthday."

All paper was stripped from incoming packages to prevent the entry of illegal messages. Labels were removed from canned goods, wrapping removed from fruit, and boxes of chocolates were emptied on the counter so the paper cups could be discarded. The only way the men were allowed to retrieve the candy was to scoop it up in their caps, and receiving it in such a manner so diminished the joy of having it that my father soon asked us not to send any more.

It wasn't until the day before Christmas that their personal effects were released and my father could at last write with his pen instead of with a pencil. He was also allowed to have up to $15 of his cash. The government issued candy and nuts to the men, but our package was the only one that arrived in time for Christmas at my father's barrack, and he told us they saved every tag and string and scrap of wrapping paper to tack up on the walls for Christmas cheer.

Soon after the men arrived in Missoula, the temperature plunged to thirty below zero. Windows were coated with ice and giant icicles hung from the roof to the ground. The men, with their California clothing, were scarcely prepared for this kind of harsh weather and finally after a month the Army issued them some basic winter clothing. We had also spent many of our evenings knitting in order to rush some wool gloves, socks, and caps to Papa and his Mitsui friends, along with books, games, and candy. He thanked us many times for everything, saying they had warmed his heart as well as his person. "The other men envy me," he wrote, "and want me to stay here forever as long as I have such a nice family!"

Early each morning, the men gathered for group calisthenics, then they worked at their assigned tasks, attended classes, and maintained a disciplined, busy life. In the evenings, when there were no meetings, they often gathered around the coal stove in the center of each barrack to socialize.

On January 3, which was my parents' twenty-fifth wedding anniversary, we sent my father a wire with our love and good wishes. He immediately wired back, "Thanks for telegram. Extend my fondest greetings on our anniversary which almost slipped my mind as I was busy arranging seventeen speakers for tomorrow's services. Everybody well and happy. Regards to church friends. Love to all."

It sounded like Papa. We were glad to know he was keeping busy and well. Our wire, it seemed, had done more than remind him of his anniversary. It had also spread the news among his friends, and that night the men of his barrack gathered around their pot-bellied stove and had a fine party in his honor. They made Japanese broth by boiling water in an old kerosene can and then adding seasoning and squares of toasted rice cakes which had been sent to one of the men. Papa's friends from other barracks came to join in the celebration, and the ensuing festivities with much singing and speech-making touched and cheered my father immensely. He wrote us about the happy evening, and the fifty or more men who were at the party sent their greetings to my mother on the back of an old Christmas card. That card and news of the celebration in Montana gave my mother as much pleasure, I think, as the flowers from my sister and me.

All during the war years my father never forgot his friends who were not as fortunate as he and had to remain in the prisoner of war camps. They were eventually scattered to distant camps in New Mexico, Louisiana, North Dakota, and Ellis Island, and some men were moved so often that letters to them would return covered with forwarding addresses that had failed to locate them. The thought of their lonely lives in internment always saddened us.

Plate in hand,
I stand in line,
Losing my resolve
To hide my tears.

⌒⌒⌒

I see my mother
In the aged woman
     who comes,
And I yield to her
My place in line.

⌒⌒⌒

Four months have passed,
And at last I learn
To call this horse stall
My family's home.

Yukari

6. Tanforan: City behind Barbed Wire

On our third Sunday in camp, we had our first visitors from outside, one of my father's business friends and his wife. A messenger came to notify us of their arrival, and we hurried to the administration building to meet them, since visitors were not permitted beyond that point.

"What can we do to help?" they asked us. "Let us know if there is anything at all we can do."

They were the first of many non-Japanese friends who came to see us offering their concern, support, and encouragement. All of them came laden with such welcome snacks as cookies, cakes, candy, potato chips, peanut butter, and fruit. We were enormously grateful for these gifts and for other packages that came through the mail (all examined before we received them), for they not only gladdened our hearts, they supplemented our meager camp diet. Some friends came faithfully every week, standing in line from one to three hours for a pass to come inside the gates.

Packages from our friends outside enabled many of us to indulge in late evening snack parties which were popular and frequent. The heavy use of hot plates put such a strain on the circuits, however, that entire barracks and stables were sometimes plunged into sudden and total darkness, causing a hasty unplugging by all concerned.

Every weekend and often even during the week, the grandstand visiting room was crowded with throngs of outside visitors. When we had no visitors of our own, my friends and I would sometimes go to the grandstand just to watch the people coming and going, for even though they were strangers to us, seeing them gave us a brief sense of contact with the outside world.

Our own visitors included not only my father's business associates, but our neighbors, my piano teacher, my mother's former Doshisha teacher who now lived in California, and many church and university people we had known over the years. One day the head of the Northern California Congregational Conference came to see us, as did on other days the chairman of the Pacific Coast Committee on American Principles and Fair Play, Dr. Galen M. Fisher (a good friend of my father's); the associate dean of women at the University of California (she had been on the same ship with us when we returned from our trip to Japan); the secretary of the YWCA; and others associated with social action groups. They came because they were our friends, but also because they were vitally concerned over the incarceration of one group of American citizens on the basis of race, and the denial of our constitutional rights.

When the evacuation took place, one of the first committees formed was the Committee on American Principles and Fair Play founded by Dr. Fisher. Its purpose was "to support the principles enunciated in the Constitution of the United States . . . and to maintain unimpaired the liberties guaranteed in the Bill of Rights, particularly for persons of Oriental ancestry." The members of this committee realized that the deprivation of the rights of one minority undermined the rights of the majority as well, and set a dangerous precedent for the future.

Dr. Fisher worked hard to dispel the false rumors of sabotage and to deny the many untruths that were circulating about Japanese Americans. He wrote several articles for the *Christian Century* as well as other publications, and along with many other educators and church leaders he realized the importance of getting the Nisei, particularly the students, back into schools as soon as possible in communities acceptable to the War Department. To accomplish this, a Student Relocation Committee was organized in Berkeley under the leadership of the YMCA-YWCA, several university presidents, other educators, and church leaders. This group was extremely helpful in assisting students to leave the "assembly centers."

In May, the Student Relocation Committee merged with other groups working on this issue, and under the aegis of the American Friends

Service Committee (a body that worked tirelessly for the Japanese Americans throughout the war) formed the National Japanese American Student Relocation Council, later headquartered in Philadelphia.

Our visitors were not only those from outside the barbed wire. Just as Japanese American friends had frequently come to our home in Berkeley, we now had visits from fellow internees who stopped by our stall at all hours of the day. It would have been impossible to avoid anyone had I wanted to, and there were times when I felt smothered. Leaving our stall brought no relief, for wherever I went there were familiar faces, everyone eager to pass the time in conversation. Until recreational activities got under way, the internees had plenty of time and no place to go.

Almost every night our stall was crowded with friends of all ages, and my mother served tea made on our hot plate and whatever food we had to share. When the neighboring stalls grew dark, however, we lowered our voices, and when Papa stood up and said, *"Sah,* it's ten o'clock," everyone left promptly. He was still very much the head of our house.

As soon as we entered Tanforan, the need for certain institutions to serve the community of 8,000 people was immediately apparent, and an interdenominational Christian church and a Buddhist church were among the first to be established. The need for spiritual sustenance brought overwhelming numbers of people to the Tanforan churches, and the first few Sundays there was standing room only at both the Japanese and English services.

A post office was opened quite early, and a hospital staffed by competent internee doctors and nurses functioned immediately and was always filled. A library was also set up and at first contained only forty-one books, but through contributions from outside eventually housed over five thousand. We also had a camp newspaper called the *Tanforan Totalizer,* published by the internees.

Another immediate and urgent need was for organized recreation and education programs, and a call for leaders and workers in these two areas was promptly answered. Within weeks, several recreation centers had been opened in the camp, and they developed a remarkable array of activities for the old as well as the young. Hundreds of players were organized into one hundred and ten softball teams and played to crowds of thousands, who had a ready-made grandstand from which to watch the games. There were also weekly musicales, talent shows, Town Hall discussions, recorded classical music concerts, Saturday night dances, hobby shows, a music school, and an art school whose six hundred students sent their work outside on exhibit. Special programs were planned for holidays, and by mid-August full length films were acquired. The first shown was "Spring Parade" with Deanna Durbin, which could be seen by anyone willing to stand in line to get in and sit on the floor to watch it. Hundreds were willing to put up with the discomfort in order to be entertained for an hour or two.

The occasional hobby shows sponsored by the Recreation Department revealed more concretely than anything else the ingenuity, patience, and skill of the Japanese Americans. Working largely with discarded scrap lumber, metal, and nails that they found on the grounds, they handcrafted objects of great beauty. In addition, they made such functional items as bookends, trays, chests, bath clogs, ashtrays, and hats woven from grasses that grew in the camp grounds. They also made good use of the manure-rich soil, cultivating flowers for pleasure and vegetables to supplement their camp diet. They built wooden boats to sail on the small lake in front of the grandstand, and the women knitted a variety of fancy sweaters and dresses with yarn ordered by mail. By September the hobby show had grown so large, a separate exhibit had to be organized for the garden and flower enthusiasts.

My sister was asked to help organize a nursery school in a small four-room cottage at the southern end of camp, and for the first time since graduating from Mills College, she was able to put to use some of her professional skills. We never learned what purpose the small cottage had served at the racetrack, but it was filthy and in a state of terrible disrepair. My sister recruited several friends, and I joined them for an entire day to scrub the dirt and grime from the floors, walls, and windows. We put up pictures cut out from old magazines, installed hooks for the children's coats, and somehow secured furniture suitable for the small children.

The morning we opened, there was a downpour and the roads were a muddy mess. This school was to service only the children from nearby barracks and that stormy morning only ten made an appearance. Eventually, as more space was acquired and additional teachers recruited, three more nursery schools were opened throughout the center, and I eventually became an assistant at one of them.

For many of the Japanese, this was the first exposure to a nursery school experience, and the adults were often as difficult to handle as the children. The first few days at my nursery school were sheer bedlam. Nearly all twenty children present were crying, some lost their breakfast, some wet their pants, and others ran into the yard screaming for their mamas. As the din increased, nearby adults came to the fence to view our efforts with amusement or indignation. "Let the poor children go on home," some shouted at us.

After a few weeks, however, both children and adults took more kindly to the nursery school routine, and soon children were coming in increasing numbers. Their mothers must have been grateful to have them out from underfoot, and the children learned to share the few toys and play things that had been secured with the help of my sister's professor at Mills College. Whenever the children played house, they always stood in line to eat at make-believe mess halls rather than cooking and setting tables as they would have done at home. It was sad to see how quickly the concept of home had changed for them.

Although I worked hard at the nursery school, I never felt quite at ease with the crying children and the wet pants, and I was devastated when two children among a group I took for a morning walk decided to defect and run for home. It was apparent my talents were not suited to nursery school teaching, and as soon as elementary schools were scheduled to open, I applied for a job as teacher in the elementary school system at a salary of $16 a month for a forty-four-hour week. The pay scale for the Japanese internees working at Tanforan was $8, $12, and $16 a month, depending on the nature of the work performed.

Three weeks after we had entered Tanforan, registration was held for school children aged six to eighteen, who by then were anxious to have some orderly routine to give substance to their long days. Four schools for grades one through three were opened in various sections of the camp and an internee teacher with elementary school credentials was in charge of each one. I was assigned to assist at one of these schools and our first classes were held on May 26. When I arrived at the school barrack at 8:30 A.M., the children were already clamoring to get in. Our first day went remarkably well, although we had no supplies or equipment for teaching and all we could do was tell stories and sing with the children.

Classes were soon separated by grade, and because of the shortage of credentialed teachers, I was placed in charge of a second grade class. We taught classes in the morning and attended meetings in the afternoon, not only to plan lessons for the next day, but to put in our time for a forty-four-hour week. The day I took over my second grade, however, I had to dismiss the children early because the building we used was also occupied by the Buddhist church on Sundays and was needed that day for the first funeral to take place in camp.

Although I had acquired some experience as an assistant, when I was on my own, my methods were of necessity empirical, and I taught mostly by instinct. The children, however, were affectionate and devoted, and it didn't take them long to discover where I lived. Each morning I would find a covey of them clustered in front of my stall, and, like the Pied Piper, I would lead them to the school barrack. When school was over, many would wait until I was ready to leave and escort me back home.

I loved teaching and decided I would like to work for a teaching credential, for I now had received my degree from the university. My classmates and I had missed commencement by two weeks and my diploma, rolled in a cardboard container, had been handed to me in my horse stall by the Tanforan mailman. The winner of the University Medal that year was a Nisei who also missed commencement because, as the president of the university stated at the ceremonies, "his country has called him elsewhere."

Gradually, supplies and books for our schools trickled in from the outside. I wrote to a former teacher with whom I had kept in touch, and she responded immediately with materials to assist me in my new occupation. Old textbooks came in from schools of the surrounding area, and one day as I helped sort a box of newly arrived books, I came across one from my old junior high school containing my own name. It was a poignant moment to come upon this dim echo of the past as I searched for material for my strange racetrack classroom.

Classes for grades four through six began soon after our school opened, and by mid-June classes through high school were in session, many of them meeting by the pari-mutuel windows beneath the grandstand. All of the classes were taught by internee instructors, as there was a sizable proportion of college graduates and a good sprinkling of Phi Beta Kappas in the Tanforan population. On the strength of their work while at Tanforan, 90 percent of the children were advanced to the next grade by the schools they had attended before the evacuation.

By the end of June, 40 percent of the residents of Tanforan were either teaching or going to school, and the education department's activities were extended to include classes in flower arrangement and first aid, and academic courses for adults as well.

During our school's existence at Tanforan, we held several Open Houses (parent attendance was well over 75 percent), issued report cards, organized PTA groups, met with parents, took children to campwide activities, and participated in such programs as the Flag Day ceremony. For their part in the Flag Day program, the children of my class sang "America the Beautiful," and many of them came combed, scrubbed, and wearing their best clothes for the occasion. A child led the audience in the pledge of allegiance to the flag, and just as they had done in school outside, the children recited the words eagerly, unaware of the irony of what they were saying. In spite of the circumstances under which the program was being held, I don't think the children had any other thought than to do honor to the flag of their country.

Other mass activities did not always go so smoothly. A marionette show to which I brought my class turned into an uproarious madhouse as three hundred school children were herded into one barrack and seated on the floor, where a few "did toilet right here," as one of my startled youngsters informed me. Our motives were good, but the lack of proper facilities often resulted in chaos that very nearly obliterated our efforts to bring the children a happy occasion.

Although we were not many miles from our old home in Berkeley, the weather at Tanforan seemed entirely alien to the usually mild Bay Area. Because of the openness of the 118 acres which constituted the racetrack and the lack of any protective buildings around it, the north wind tore through the camp each day, sweeping with it the loose dirt of the track and its surrounding grounds. Even the sun seemed harsher and less benevolent than it had back home. There was much illness and the schools were constantly staffed by substitute teachers as one or another of the regular teachers fell ill.

I developed red splotches on my hands, diagnosed by the doctors as a Vitamin B deficiency, and finally caught a bad cold that kept me in my stall for several days. I knew what my unfortunate substitute had put up with when one of my children stopped by to visit me. He produced a large sheet of paper with the word "boy" scribbled all over it and told me proudly, "I was class monitor and wrote down 'boy' everytime one was bad."

All of us, especially my mother, were troubled by frequent stomach disorders, and my sister, who until now had always been the healthy one in the family, caught a bad cold from which she didn't recover for over a month. For many days she had to stay in bed in the dark windowless half of our stall with just enough of a temperature to preclude her going out.

On days when I was also sick, we shared the misery of "the dungeon" together, emerging into the front section for a half hour each evening when a small patch of sunshine entered our stall. Sometimes Issei friends would come to call on my sister, offering home-made remedies and even unwanted massages. With no place to hide, she had to endure their well-meaning efforts, when more than anything she just wanted to be left alone.

We carried all her meals to her from the mess hall on trays, but her greatest problem was in not being able to walk to the latrine. It was simple enough to find a makeshift bedpan, but it was embarrassing for her to use it, knowing the neighbors could hear everything but the faintest of sighs. We finally solved the problem by keeping newspapers on hand, and it was my function during her illness to rattle them vigorously and noisily whenever she used the bedpan. It was a relief to both of us when she finally recovered.

Over the weeks the food improved considerably, and our mess hall workers, all internees also earning the minimal government pay, made special efforts to please us by making doughnuts for breakfast or biscuits for dinner. In appreciation, the families who shared our mess hall collected $83 to present to them. They in turn put flowers on the tables and baked a beautiful cake for dessert. While we were basking in this exchange of mutual regard at our mess hall, a friend told me that the Army had come to take films of her mess hall, removing the Japanese cooks and replacing them with white cooks for the occasion. She was so infuriated by this deception that she refused to go to her mess hall to eat while the films were being made. It was hard to understand just what the Army was trying to prove.

As our physical needs were met, and recreational and educational programs organized, the internees proceeded to establish some form of self-government. A council was established, composed of representatives from the five precincts into which the "assembly center" was divided. Nineteen candidates filed petitions to run for the five council posts and a full-fledged political campaign ensued, with parades, posters, campaign speeches, and door-to-door calls.

This was the first opportunity for the Issei to cast a vote in the United States. Although there had been test cases, the Supreme Court had ruled that they were ineligible for citizenship, and it was not until 1952 that legislation was passed making it possible for them to become naturalized. The Issei did not waste the opportunity that came their way inside the barbed wire. Much to their credit, they outvoted their Nisei children four to one, and elected the candidates of their choice.

Franchise for the Issei, however, was short-lived, for only a month later the Army issued a directive that limited voting and office-holding to American citizens only. The Issei accepted this ruling stoically and calmly, just as they had borne every other restriction that had been placed on their lives since they had come to the United States.

Toward the end of July, a constitution was approved and thirty-eight candidates were elected to a legislative congress in a quiet, orderly election. All of this proved to be quite meaningless, however, for soon thereafter the Army dissolved all "assembly center" self-governmental bodies. No one was particularly disturbed by this order, because by then interest in politics had subsided considerably. The first rumors of an impending inland move had already begun to circulate, and we knew our unique racetrack community would soon be defunct.

On June 19 a "head count" was instituted and each day, at the sound of a siren, we were required to be in our quarters before breakfast and again at 6:30 P.M. It seemed an unnecessary irritation to add to our lives, unless it was designed to impress on us the fact that we were under surveillance, for there was little opportunity or inclination for anyone to escape. A deputy was appointed in each barrack or stable to knock on every door, and we were required to respond by calling out the number of occupants present. It was a ridiculous procedure, and I sometimes shouted "none" instead of "four" when our deputy came knocking. Our "headcounter" took his job very seriously, however, and never appreciated my flippant attitude.

Two months after our arrival, lights were put up outside our barracks, giving the entire camp the air of a Japanese village and making the night seem more benign. It also made nighttime trips to the latrine and washroom safer, although we never made such trips alone. I often dreamed at night, and in my dreams I was always home in Berkeley. I never dreamed of Tanforan, and it was always disappointing to open my eyes in the fading darkness, see the coarse stable roof over my head, and realize that the horse stall was my present reality.

The FBI, which had already made its presence acutely felt in our family, now made an appearance in our camp. On June 23, FBI agents instituted a campwide search for contraband, turning some stalls inside out while scarcely disturbing others, depending largely on the mood and nature of the agent making the search. Whether cursory or thorough, however, the effect on morale was uniformly bad throughout the camp.

Rumors of our removal to inland "relocation centers" continued to circulate, and there was much speculation as to where we would be sent. Although we knew that Tanforan was only a temporary home, we all worked constantly to make the windswept racetrack a more attractive and pleasant place. Dozens of small vegetable and flower gardens flourished along the barracks and stables, and a corner of camp that once housed a junk pile was transformed into a colorful camp garden of stocks, sweetpeas, irises, zinnias, and marigolds. A group of talented men also made a miniature park with trees and a waterfall, creating a small lake complete with a wooden bridge, a pier, and an island. It wasn't much, but it was one of the many efforts made to comfort the eye and heart.

On July 11 we were issued our first scrip books with which we could buy anything sold at the camp Canteen. A single person was issued a book for $2.50, while a married couple received $4. This was our allotment for one month, but since scrip books hadn't been issued in June, we were to receive a two-month supply. We stood in line for over two hours, and my sister and I each received $5 and my parents $8. It seemed a great windfall suddenly to have $5 to spend, but when Kay and I hurried to the Canteen there was nothing left to buy. The ice cream, Cracker Jack, candy, peanuts, and shoe laces were all sold out.

Also in July we were each given $14 as a clothing allowance, and for the first time in my life, I was introduced to the fascination of poring through a Montgomery Ward catalogue to see what $14 could buy.

In mid-July, paychecks covering the period from our first day of work to June 21 were issued. Once more I stood in a long line and waited for hours to receive my check. It was from the United States Treasury Department for the sum of $6.38. I wondered how this miserly sum had been determined, but was hardly in a position to bargain for anything better. It was slightly better than nothing at all, and I was pleased to have my first paycheck. The next month my check climbed to $16, the maximum rate for professionals, and I also received another scrip book for $2.50. This time when I went to the Canteen, I was able to buy some Cracker Jack and candy.

In late summer a laundry and barbershop were added to the services available, but by then we had become used to doing without such luxuries. Most people continued to do their own wash, and my mother, who had ordered scissors and clippers by mail, gave my father all his haircuts, a service she continued to perform even after they left camp.

As the summer days lengthened, my friends and I would often go for walks after supper. Following the curve of the racetrack, we would gravitate without thought to the grandstand where we would climb to the highest seats to get a glimpse of the world beyond the barbed wire. We could see the cars on Skyline Boulevard, over which we had traveled so many times, and we could see planes taking off from Moffett Field, soaring toward the Pacific with graceful precision. Beyond were the coastline hills reflecting the warm glow of sunset before turning a deep, dark blue. For a while we would talk about our fun-filled prewar days, but eventually we would lapse into silence and sit in the growing darkness of evening, each of us nurturing our own private longings and hopes.

All of us waited eagerly for mail, for many of our friends were in other "assembly centers" and some had moved to inland areas of California during the time when the so-called "voluntary evacuation" was permitted. Such "voluntary" moves within California had proved to be completely futile, however, for the Army promptly extended its exclusion zones. Friends who had moved from Zone One to Reedley, where they thought they would be safe, soon found themselves subject to removal after all, and were eventually sent to a camp in Arizona. Had they not attempted the first move at all, they could have been with their Bay Area friends in Tanforan, and later Topaz, and saved themselves considerable expense as well.

Other friends joined four families and moved to Gilroy in April, presuming they would be safe there from removal and internment. The men worked days on a Japanese American peach ranch and spent their evenings hastily constructing communal living quarters. In July, however, the exclusion zones were extended, and with time only to board up their newly built shelter, all the families, including the ranch owner, were forced to move to the Tule Lake camp. When, after the war, my friends returned to Gilroy, they could find neither the house they had built nor anything the group had left inside. Everything had disappeared without a trace.

Life at Tanforan was not without its comical aspects. One afternoon our neighbor rushed back from the Canteen and knocked on our door, beaming.

"I found some paper napkins," she explained with obvious delight. "There was a terrible crowd pushing and shoving to get them, but I picked up a box for you too."

My mother thanked her for her thoughtfulness, and they opened their packages together. It was only then that our neighbor learned she had purchased sanitary, not paper, napkins, and she told us through tears of laughter that most of the eager buyers had been men from the bachelor quarters. We hoped they had had time to examine their boxes before taking them to the mess hall for dinner, and I certainly wished I could have seen their faces when they did.

After three months of communal living, the lack of privacy began to grate on my nerves. There was no place I could go to be completely alone—not in the washroom, the latrine, the shower, or my stall. I couldn't walk down the track without seeing someone I knew. I couldn't avoid the people I didn't like or choose those I wished to be near. There was no place to cry and no place to hide. It was impossible to escape from the constant noise and human presence. I felt stifled and suffocated and sometimes wanted to scream. But in my family we didn't scream or cry or fight or even have a major argument, because we knew the neighbors were always only inches away.

When a vacancy occurred in a stall a few doors down, my sister and I immediately applied for permission to move into it. We all needed the additional space, for we had had just about all the togetherness we could stand for a while. My father and our friends helped us make shelves, a table, and a bench from scrap lumber, and my sister and I finally had a place of our own. Now each morning and evening it was our luxury to be able to call out "two" instead of "four" to the "head-counter."

The artist who lived a few stalls down tried to solve her need for privacy by tacking a large "Quarantined—Do Not Enter" sign on her door. But rather than keeping people away, it only drew further attention to her reluctant presence.

"What's wrong with you?" her friends would call.

And she would shout back, "Hoof and mouth disease. Go away!"

During the first few days in camp, my mother tried to achieve some privacy and rest by having us padlock the door from the outside as Kay and I went off with our friends. But we realized this was dangerous in case of fire, and she eventually resigned herself to the open communal life. It wasn't easy for her, however, as she longed for quiet moments to rest and reflect and write her poetry. Such moments were difficult if not impossible to come by in camp, and the more sensitive a person was, the more he or she suffered. Knitting was one thing that could be done even with people around, so my mother did a great deal of it and made some beautiful sweaters for my sister and me.

Although we worked hard at our jobs to keep Tanforan functioning properly, we also sought to forestall the boredom of our confinement by keeping busy in a number of other ways. My sister and I both took first aid classes and joined the church choir, which once collaborated with the Little Theater group to present the works of Stephen Foster, complete with sets that featured a moving steamboat. We also went to some of the dances where decorations festooned the usually bleak hall at the grandstand and music was provided by a band made up of internee musicians. When I had time, I also went to art class and did some paintings so I would have a visual record of our life at Tanforan. I was surprised and pleased one day when I went to a hobby show and saw a second place red ribbon pinned to one of my paintings.

One of the elementary school teachers was the first to be married at Tanforan. She wanted, understandably, to have the kind of wedding she would have had on the outside, and wore a beautiful white marquisette gown with a fingertip veil. For all of us who crowded into the church barrack that day, the wedding was a moment of extraordinary joy and brightness. We showered the couple with rice as they left, and they climbed into a borrowed car decorated with "just married" signs and a string of tin cans. They took several noisy turns around the racetrack in the car and then, after a reception in one of the recreation centers, began their married life in one of the horse stalls.

On August 19 the supervisor of elementary education asked us to write summary reports of our class activities for the War Relocation Authority in preparation for closing our schools. This was the first concrete indication we had that we would soon be leaving for inland "relocation centers," and we were relieved that the endless speculation was about to end. Still, it was not an official announcement and we were not told where we would be going, although Utah had been mentioned most frequently.

Three days later it was officially announced that we would be moved sometime between September 15 and 30. Now we knew the date, but we still did not know our destination. We were told we would be moved in small contingents, with mess hall areas as the basis for division, and new rumors began to float that our mess hall unit would be the first to leave.

On August 24 our evening roll call period was extended, and we were required to remain in our quarters for over an hour while a camp-wide inventory of government property took place. Most of us had no government property in our stalls other than the cots, mattresses, and light bulbs that were there the day we arrived.

Soon the ever present rumors began to take on a new shape. We heard our mess hall would not be leaving first after all; that our camp might be split up, separating us from our friends; and that we might be sent to Idaho instead of Utah. But we weren't too concerned about our destination, for one place was as remote and unknown to us as the next. It was the uncertainty that made everyone nervous and anxious to trade rumors, and it wasn't long before tempers began to flare over trivial matters.

September 4 was the last day of school, and my final paycheck was for $13.76. I had been docked for being sick and for a two-day vacation given to all of us in August. We were also to be issued another scrip book, but when my father and I went to pick ours up, the line was so long, we decided it wasn't worth the wait.

On the final day of school we invited the parents to a special program of songs, recitations, and refreshments, and our custodian distributed a box of butterballs to the children as his parting gift. We said our brief farewells and then returned to our barracks to worry about the Army inspection for contraband that was scheduled for the following day.

The inspection was to begin at 8:00 A.M., and we were told to remain in our quarters until it was completed. We waited in our stall until 11:00, but not one soldier made an appearance. Thinking it might be hours before they arrived, Kay and I risked a quick trip to the laundry to do a wash. We hurriedly hung it up on our outside lines, but the wind covered everything with dust, leaving us ill-rewarded for our efforts and more frustrated than ever. We ate a hurried lunch and then returned once more to our stalls to wait. In the meantime, the inevitable rumors began to travel. The soldiers were late, people said, because they were confiscating all sorts of items throughout camp, and we grew increasingly jittery as we wondered what the soldiers would do when they finally arrived.

At last, at 4:00 P.M., fifteen soldiers appeared and stood guard around our entire stable. They obeyed orders with such rigidity that two women who happened to be in the latrine when the soldiers arrived were not permitted to return to their own stalls. One MP and one plainclothesman then proceeded to enter each stall to make the search. By the time they finally reached us, however, they were so tired they made only a cursory survey of our possessions and left quickly after exchanging a few friendly words. "All that worry for nothing," I grumbled. We had had nothing to hide or to be confiscated, but it was simply not knowing what to expect that had been the worst of it. And we had, by now, been conditioned to be apprehensive of anything the Army did.

Since all camp activities had been suspended for the day, visitors too had been barred, and we learned later that our Swiss neighbors had come all the way from Berkeley and been turned away. They were determined to see us, however, and returned the next day laden with snacks and some of my mother's London Smoke carnations, the stems carefully wrapped in wet cotton. Because their two boys were under sixteen, they were not permitted to enter the grounds, and when Kay and I went outside to look for them, we saw them standing disconsolately near the gate.

"Teddy! Bobby!" I called out, and they came running toward us, thrusting their hands through the wire fencing. We tried to shake their hands and had just begun an eager exchange of news when an armed guard approached, shouting, "Hey, get away from the fence, you two!"

My sister and I backed away quickly, and our brief visit came to an abrupt, frustrating end. The boys later told me they had never forgotten the incident, for they thought at the time the guards were going to shoot us.

With a departure date set, we began once more the onerous task of packing our possessions. Although we now had considerably fewer things than when we left Berkeley, the confusion and disarray were still massive. This time a canvas "camp bundle" wouldn't do, for our belongings were to be shipped by train to Utah and required sturdier containers. But this time we had Papa, and he disassembled everything our friends had built for us when we first arrived. He saved every scrap of wood and every nail, and converted our shelves, tables, and benches into shipping crates. The sound of hammering filled the length of the stable as everyone felt once more the urgent need to be ready when the Army gave the word to move.

On September 9 the first contingent from Tanforan was scheduled to leave for the Central Utah Relocation Center. I was glad we were not among this pioneering group for I was not eager to leave California. Our laundry barrack was designated as the point of departure, and the entire area surrounding it was fenced off to provide a place for baggage inspection before the people boarded a train that was pulled up to a siding at the edge of camp. The departure had been timed for the dinner hour so the departing group could slip away without creating a major commotion, but most of us managed to rush through supper and hurry back to the barricade to say goodbye to our friends.

We all wanted to do something to ease the pain of still another uprooting for those about to leave, and while we could only be supportive by our presence, one of the Japanese maintenance men found another way. He appeared with a wheelbarrow full of bright flowers from the camp garden, and gave bouquets to any who could reach out a hand through the barricade to accept his gift. A large crowd had gathered to watch the proceedings, but was temporarily dispersed when the siren signaled the 6:30 head count. The minute we were counted, however, we all ran back to watch for as long as we could, waving and shouting to give our friends a rousing send-off.

It seemed everyone wanted to do a final wash before leaving for Utah and the washtubs were in constant use. My mother spent an entire morning washing clothes and sheets, not even bothering to eat breakfast because she would have lost the tub had she left it. Hot water was still scarce and we still had to carry bucketfuls from the washroom, for the laundry barracks had shown no improvement since the early days of camp life.

Gradually our life at Tanforan was drawing to a close. My father collected a fund from residents in our area for the mess hall crew, and they in turn converted it into cakes and ice cream for a farewell dinner in our small mess hall.

Two days before we were to leave, an inspection of our freight baggage was scheduled. Again we waited for most of the day, but the inspector didn't arrive until just before our 4:00 P.M. supper shift at the main mess hall. He stopped a frustrating four stalls away, and our inspection was put off until the following day.

We should, by then, have been used to long waits and delays, but each time it was unnerving and unpleasant. When the inspection finally took place, it was a mere formality, and trucks then came to pick up our baggage for shipment to our new home. It wouldn't be long before we, too, would be heading for what was then officially called the Central Utah Relocation Center.

7. Topaz: City of Dust

On the sixteenth of September, our family was assigned to Group IV of the four groups departing that day for Delta, Utah. We were to have supper at 4:00 P.M. and be at the departure point by 5:00 P.M., but we had no appetite at such an early hour and were too nervous to eat.

Friends who were leaving at a later date, came to help us carry our many suitcases and bundles and to see us off at the departure area. Our bedding, which we had used until the night before and would need again as soon as we arrived in Utah, made up our bulkiest bundle. Stuffing last minute articles into knitting bags and purses, and feeling somewhat like refugees carrying our worldly possessions, we hurried to the departure point for the inspection of our baggage.

Our bedding was checked first and tossed through a window into the laundry barrack, already crowded with earlier arrivals. After our hand baggage was checked we went inside, were told to sit in alphabetical order in Group IV, and waited for what seemed several hours. I stood on a bench and looked out the window hoping to catch a glimpse of the friends who had come to see us off, but I could see only a mass of faces. It appeared the entire camp had come to watch our departure. Finally it was time to leave and we walked single file between a double row of MPs and were counted as we boarded the train. Invalids and disabled people were placed in two Pullman cars attached at the rear.

About 8:00 P.M. the train, loaded with five hundred internees, was ready at last to begin its journey to Utah. We all clustered at the windows for a final look at Tanforan, scanning the crowds for friends staying behind. There were people gathered along the fence, on rooftops, on barrack steps, any place where they could get a glimpse of the train. They shouted and waved as though they would not see us for a long time, although they knew they would be following us in just a few weeks.

It had only been a crude community of stables and barracks, but it had been home for five months and we had grown accustomed to our life there. Now it was another wrench, another uprooting, and this time we were bound for an unknown and forbidding destination. Those who remained seemed to watch us go with the same apprehension we felt. Neither side quite wanted to let go. We waved to each other as long as we could, and those of us on the train pressed up to the windows, holding close the final sight of all that was familiar. The last thing we saw as the train pulled out was a group of teenagers who had climbed to the roof of one of the barracks. They were waving and holding aloft an enormous banner on which they had painted, "So long for a while, Utah bound."

Long after Tanforan disappeared, we were still staring out the windows, for now we were seeing all the things we had missed for five months—houses, gardens, stores, cars, traffic lights, dogs, white children—and of course no one wanted to miss seeing San Francisco Bay and the bay bridge. We were told the shades must be drawn from sunset to sunrise, and it had already grown dark. By the time we passed the bay, we could only look out from the edge of the drawn shades, but we could see the lights of the bridge sparkling across the dark water, still serene and magnificent and untouched by the war. I continued to look out long after the bridge had vanished into the darkness, unutterably saddened by this fleeting glimpse of all that meant home to me.

The train was an old model, undoubtedly released from storage for wartime use. It was fitted with fixtures for gas lights, and the seats were as hard and straight-backed as old church pews.

Sleep came only fitfully the first night, for the car was full of restless people, some of whom had never ridden on a train before. The water container was soon emptied, some people became trainsick, and the condition of the washroom was enough to discourage more than the fainthearted. We waited eagerly for morning, and breakfast cheered our sagging spirits. We ate at 7:00 on the first shift, and although the plates were paper, it felt good to sit once more at a cloth-covered table, on chairs instead of benches, and to use some nice silverware. The food was plentiful and tasted good. The waiters who served it were courteous and we took up a collection in our car to tip them properly. There were only two diners for five hundred people, however, so the last group, who didn't breakfast until 11:00, may not have fared as well.

By noon we were traveling through Nevada sagebrush country, and when we reached a properly isolated area, the train came to a stop. Our car captain then announced that we could get off for a half hour break in the fresh air. As we stepped down from the car, we found that armed MPs had stationed themselves in a row parallel to the train. Only if we remained in the narrow corridor between them and the train were we allowed to stay outside. Some people ran back and forth, some did calisthenics, and others just breathed in the dry desert air.

We were also permitted two daytime visits to other cars during one-hour visiting periods, and my father, sister, and I walked the length of the twelve cars as much for exercise as to find our friends, but my mother was too tired to join us. At 5:00 P.M. there was a head count and at 7:00 the lights were turned on and the shades drawn until dawn the following morning.

By the second night, we were so stiff and numb, sleep was out of the question for all of us, and the heaters that had been activated added to our discomfort. I wasn't anxious to get to Topaz, but I could hardly wait to get off that lumbering train.

We crossed the Great Salt Lake about 9:30 P.M. and were given permission to turn out the lights and pull up the shades for a few minutes. The lake, shimmering in white moonlight, seemed an almost magical sight. Voices quieted down and the car became silent as we all gazed at the vast glistening body of water, forgetting for a few moments our tired, aching bodies.

When we reached the Salt Lake City station about midnight, I opened my window to look out and was astonished to see a former Nisei classmate standing on the platform.

"Helen, what in the world are you doing here?" I asked.

In a quick flurry of words she told me she had "evacuated voluntarily" to Salt Lake City and, hearing that the internee train would be passing through, had come to see if she could find any of her friends.

We talked quickly, trying to exchange news of as many mutual friends as we could in the few minutes we had. But soon it was time for our train to move on, and she clasped my hand briefly. "Good luck, Yo," she called out, and our train moved slowly out of the station with its strange cargo of internees. I envied her freedom, and it pained me to think I was about to be imprisoned, not because of anything I had done, but simply because I hadn't been able to "evacuate voluntarily" as she had done.

I had slept only two hours when the car captain woke us for a 5:00 A.M. breakfast. I straggled after my family to the diner half asleep, but was rewarded with a fine meal, this time served on china. Dawn was breaking over the desert as our family sat together in the diner, just as we had done so many times on happier occasions. For a moment I felt the faint illusion that we were once more on a vacation together, but this passed quickly. The presence of Japanese faces at every table, and the need to eat quickly and vacate our table for those still waiting, soon propelled me back to reality.

As the train approached our destination we watched the landscape closely, hoping it would give us some indication of what the Topaz "relocation center" would be like. I felt cautiously optimistic as we reached the town of Delta for the land didn't appear to be too unfriendly or barren. A cheerful man boarded the train and passed out copies of the first issue of *The Topaz Times*, which gave us instructions regarding procedures at the new camp. I could tell a public relations man was already at work for the masthead contained a picture of a faceted topaz gemstone and in large print the words, "Topaz—Jewel of the Desert."

Once more we were counted as we got off the train and then were transferred to buses for the final leg of our journey to Topaz. As we rode along, I continued to feel fairly hopeful, for we were passing small farms, cultivated fields, and clusters of trees. After a half hour, however, there was an abrupt change. All vegetation stopped. There were no trees or grass or growth of any kind, only clumps of dry skeletal greasewood.

We were entering the edge of the Sevier Desert some fifteen miles east of Delta and the surroundings were now as bleak as a bleached bone. In the distance there were mountains rising above the valley with some majesty, but they were many miles away. The bus made a turn into the heart of the sun-drenched desert and there in the midst of nowhere were rows and rows of squat, tar-papered barracks sitting sullenly in the white, chalky sand. This was Topaz, the Central Utah Relocation Center, one of ten such camps located throughout the United States in equally barren and inaccessible areas.

In April of 1942, the director of the War Relocation Authority and a representative of the Western Defense Command had met with the governors of the western states to discuss the feasibility of assisting the Japanese internees to relocate in small groups throughout the intermountain and western states. All but one of the governors opposed this plan, however, and indicated that the internees could enter their states only under strict military guard. And this was precisely how we entered the state of Utah.

As the bus drew up to one of the barracks, I was surprised to hear band music. Marching toward us down the dusty road was the drum and bugle corps of the young Boy Scouts who had come with the advance contingent, carrying signs that read, "Welcome to Topaz—Your Camp." It was a touching sight to see them standing in the burning sun, covered with dust, as they tried to ease the shock of our arrival at this desolate desert camp.

A few of our friends who had arrived earlier were also there to greet us. They tried hard to look cheerful, but their pathetic dust-covered appearance told us a great deal more than their brave words.

We went through the usual arrival procedure of registering, having a brief medical examination, and being assigned living quarters. Our family was assigned to Apartment C of Barrack 2 in Block 7, and from now on our address would be 7-2-C, Topaz, Utah. We discovered that our block was located in the northeast corner of the camp, just opposite the quarters of the Military Police and not far from the camp hospital.

The entire camp was divided into forty-two blocks, each containing twelve barracks constructed around a mess hall, a latrine-washroom,

Topaz: a cluster of dusty tar-papered barracks in the bleak Sevier Desert.
Hidden from view are the barbed wire fence and the guard towers.
Courtesy of Mr. and Mrs. Emil Sekerak

The arrival of baggage was a hectic, but eagerly awaited event in the early days at Topaz. *Courtesy of Mr. and Mrs. Emil Sekerak*

and a laundry. The camp was one mile square and eventually housed 8,000 residents, making it the fifth largest city in the state of Utah.

As we plodded through the powdery sand toward Block 7, I began to understand why everyone looked like pieces of flour-dusted pastry. In its frantic haste to construct this barrack city, the Army had removed every growing thing, and what had once been a peaceful lake bed was now churned up into one great mass of loose flour-like sand. With each step we sank two to three inches deep, sending up swirls of dust that crept into our eyes and mouths, noses and lungs. After two long sleepless nights on the train, this sudden encounter with the sun, the glaring white sand, and the altitude made me feel weak and light-headed. We were all worried about my mother, and I thought I might collapse myself, when we finally reached Block 7.

Each barrack was one hundred feet in length, and divided into six rooms for families of varying sizes. We were assigned to a room in the center, about twenty by eighteen feet, designed for occupancy by four people. When we stepped into our room it contained nothing but four army cots without mattresses. No inner sheetrock walls or ceilings had yet been installed, nor had the black pot-bellied stove that stood outside our door. Cracks were visible everywhere in the siding and around the windows, and although our friends had swept out our room before we arrived, the dust was already seeping into it again from all sides.

The instruction sheet advised us not to put up any shelves until the carpenters arrived from Tanforan to install the sheetrock walls. In fact, three paragraphs were devoted to reassuring us that plenty of scrap lumber was available and that a committee had been organized to supervise its distribution. "A rough estimate of 400,000 board feet of lumber is now available," one paragraph stated. "Since sufficient wood is available, there will be no necessity for hoarding or nocturnal commando raids."

There was also a paragraph about words. "You are now in Topaz, Utah," it read. "Here we say Dining Hall and not Mess Hall; Safety Council, not Internal Police; Residents, not Evacuees; and last but not least, Mental Climate, not Morale." After our long and exhausting ordeal, a patronizing sheet of instructions was the last thing we needed.

It also told us there would be four bathtubs for the women in each block, flush toilets and individual basins in all washrooms. This I had to see. On my quick tour of inspection I discovered the toilets had no seats, there was no water in the laundry, and the lights didn't work in the showers or latrines. Our water was pumped up from nearby artesian wells almost 1,000 feet deep, and twice during our first day the water was shut off completely.

The first lunch served in our mess hall seemed adequate, but our Japanese American chef felt he hadn't prepared a meal worthy of a welcome. He came from the kitchen to apologize personally for the meager fare, explaining he couldn't do better because he lacked provisions as well as help. Apparently everything, including food and personnel, was still in extremely short supply.

We returned to our room after lunch, and although our mattresses hadn't yet been delivered, we were so exhausted we lay down on the springs of our army cots and slept all afternoon. When I woke up, my mouth tasted of dust.

That evening our project director, Charles F. Ernst, came to our block to speak to us. We met in the mess hall and he introduced several of the thirty white administrative heads (civil service employees) who were in charge of various camp functions. He seemed a kind and understanding man of considerable warmth and left us feeling sufficiently heartened to face the next day.

The temperature the next morning was well below freezing. A thin layer of ice had formed in the kettle of water we kept in our room, and I found it hard to get out of bed even with the importunate banging of the cook's spoon on a dishpan to tell us breakfast was ready. We soon discovered that the temperature variation in a single day could be as much as fifty degrees. Some days started at thirty degrees Fahrenheit and soared by midafternoon to the eighties and nineties, compelling us to wear winter wools in the morning and change to summer clothing by afternoon. When my sister and I went out to meet some incoming buses in the hot desert sun, we came home sunburned, covered with dust, and feeling like well-broiled meat.

My father, with his usual energy, was quick to find our block's most pressing needs and alleviate them where he could. He spent his first morning in Topaz with three men cleaning the latrines, which were in an appalling state of filth because many people had suffered food poisoning (there was no refrigeration in the kitchens) and a rash of diarrhea had resulted. Our conversations in those early days were often reduced to comparing the number of visits we had made to the latrine, and we ate our food gingerly, smelling it carefully to make sure it wasn't spoiled.

On the afternoon of his first day, my father went to the gate to meet the incoming buses, and having discovered ice cream bars at the Canteen, he distributed them to the delighted Boy Scouts who were marching again in the dust and heat to greet the incoming internees.

Although internees continued to arrive each day from Tanforan, the blocks to which they were assigned were increasingly ill-equipped to house them. People who arrived a few days after we did found gaping holes in the roof where the stove pipes were to fit, latrine barracks with no roofs at all, and mattresses filled only with straw. Those who arrived still later didn't even have barracks to go to and were simply assigned to cots set up in empty mess halls, laundries, or the corridors of the hospital. Many internees found themselves occupying barracks where hammering, tarring, and roofing were still in progress, and one unfortunate woman received second degree burns on her face when boiling tar seeped through the roof onto the bed where she was asleep.

It was inhumane and unnecessary to subject the internees to such discomfort after their grueling train ride from California, but it was too late to remedy matters. Once again the Army had sent the Japanese Americans into crude, incomplete, and ill-prepared camps.

In those first few days, camp life was too disorganized for me to apply for a job, but wanting to do something constructive with my time, I volunteered to help our block manager as secretary. His duty was to function as liaison between the residents of our block and the administration, but he actually spent most of his time listening to the many people who flocked to him with complaints. No one was happy with the housing assignments and nearly everyone wanted to move. Had the Army waited to bring us in after the barracks were reasonably comfortable, much of this distress could have been forestalled. As it was, the general sense of malaise and despair funneled itself into the mistaken belief that a move to another block would bring some improvement.

Committees mushroomed daily in the community of Topaz and one was soon created to deal specifically with housing adjustments. Its overworked members often met until 3:00 and 4:00 in the morning trying to find solutions to the overwhelming problems that inundated them. It was many weeks, however, before they even began to see any satisfactory results from their efforts.

Daytime, with its debilitating heat and the stresses of camp life, was harsh and unkind, but early evening after supper was a peaceful time of day at Topaz. The sand retained the warmth of the sun, and the moon rose from behind dark mountains with the kind of clear brilliance seen only in a vast desert sky. We often took walks along the edge of camp, watching sunsets made spectacular by the dusty haze and waiting for the moon to rise in the darkening sky. It was one of the few things to look forward to in our life at Topaz.

Sometimes as we walked, we could hear the MPs singing in their quarters and then they seemed something more than the sentries who patrolled the barbed wire perimeters of our camp, and we realized they were lonely young boys far from home too. Still, they were on the other side of the fence, and they represented the Army we had come to fear and distrust. We never offered them our friendship, although at times they tried to talk to us.

If I thought the dust I had breathed and absorbed so far was bad, I had seen nothing yet. About a week after we arrived, I encountered my first dust storm. The morning began cold and brittle as always, but by afternoon a strange warm wind had begun to blow. I happened to be in another block walking home with a friend when the wind suddenly gathered ominous strength. It swept around us in great thrusting gusts, flinging swirling masses of sand in the air and engulfing us in a thick cloud that eclipsed barracks only ten feet away.

My friend grabbed my hand and pulled me into the nearest laundry barrack, but even inside, the air was thick with dust. The flimsy structure shuddered violently with each blast of wind, and we could hear garbage cans and wooden crates being swept from the ground and slammed against the building. We waited more than an hour, silent and rigid with fear, but the storm didn't let up. I was afraid the laundry barrack might simply break apart and the howling wind would fling us out into the desert, but I was too terrified even to voice my thoughts. When at last the wind wasn't quite so shrill, we decided to run for our home barracks so we wouldn't be trapped where we were until night.

The moment I turned the knob, the wind flung the door from me, and leaning into the wind, I started off alone in the blinding dust storm. As I ran, I could feel the sand swirling into my eyes and nose and mouth. I couldn't breathe and the dust was choking me. But fear gave me strength to fight the storm and I finally reached Block 7. When I stumbled into our room, I was covered with dust. My hair, my eyelashes, and my eyebrows were white with it, and my mouth was filled with its chalky taste. I found my mother sitting alone and frightened in our dust-filled room. The air looked smoky with dust.

"Thank goodness you're safe, Yo Chan," she said. "Do you know where Kay and Papa are?"

I didn't and I wished they would get home. But I told her, "Don't worry, Mama, they're probably waiting out the storm in some safe place."

It was pointless trying to clean our room until the wind stopped blowing, so my mother and I shook out our blankets, lay down on our cots, and waited for the dust storm to subside. It was a long afternoon, and my father and sister didn't get back until suppertime. Both of them returned covered with dust and looking just as I had when I had run home.

The wind didn't die down until long after the sun had set, and when I went outside to look at the sky, it was almost as though the dust storm had been a bad dream. The air was calm and still, and the night sky was filled with a mass of stars that seemed to mock me with their piercing brilliance.

My mother and I tried to do a wash in the morning, but all the tubs were taken and the water soon ran out. We swept out our room and wiped away what dust we could, but by afternoon another wind storm blew up, so we simply covered everything with newspapers and waited for the storm to blow itself out.

Just as at Tanforan, we had to deal in our early days at Topaz with the matter of physical adjustment. Because of the daily extremes in temperature, the altitude (4,600 feet above sea level), and the ever pervasive dust, it took many weeks for us to become acclimated and to overcome the despondency caused by the inadequacy of everything from housing to food. We tried taking salt pills as the doctors suggested, but found that instead of helping matters, they simply nauseated us.

Once more my sister grew ill and spent many long days in bed, prompting a well-meaning Issei friend to bring her a small container of clear broth.

"Just take this, Keiko San," she urged, "and you'll be strong and healthy in no time at all. I guarantee it will work."

It wasn't until after Kay was up and around that the friend came again to see her. "It worked, didn't it—my broth?" she asked.

"I guess it did," my sister allowed.

Only then did the woman reveal she had made the brew with earthworms. "It's guaranteed to restore good health," she said proudly.

In a few days she came back again, this time with a small bottle of ink-black liquid. "It's essence of egg yolk," she explained. "I made it myself by rendering the oil from many egg yolks. Try it, Keiko San," she urged, "and you'll never be sick again."

But my sister had had enough of the woman's nostrums. "Thanks, but not me," she said shaking her head. And it was Mama, ever trusting and hopeful, who gave it a try. There was no great improvement in her health, but she faithfully swallowed the foul-smelling black oil for a long time before she gave up.

None of us felt well during our incarceration in Topaz. We all caught frequent colds during the harsh winter months and had frequent stomach upsets. Illness was a nuisance, especially after we began to work, for memos from a doctor were required to obtain sick leave. Much of our energy simply went into keeping our room dusted, swept, and mopped to be rid of the constant accumulation of dust, and in trying to do a laundry when the water was running.

We had no idea when the water would be turned on, for its appearance had no predictable pattern. Its stoppage was equally unpredictable, and people sometimes got caught in the shower covered with soap when the water trickled to a maddening stop. We simply had to help each other. When the water was running, a neighbor would bang on our door and shout, "The water's running." Then whoever was home at the time would rush with buckets and pans to the laundry and bring back enough water to provide an emergency supply in our room. Often we would just grab our soap and towel and run for the showers, and sometimes, in our haste, we forgot our towels and had to use our clothes to dry ourselves.

If we were lucky, Mama and I would happen on an empty laundry tub when the water was running. If in addition it was hot, we would take everything in our laundry hamper and do an enormous wash. Hand washing the bed linens, towels, and clothing for four people using only a wooden washboard was an exhausting task. My mother and I felt completely depleted after we had finished, but we were also relieved of considerable frustration, at least until our hamper was full again. And in the meantime, there was also the ironing to be done.

Water wasn't the only thing in short supply. One day there was talk that a transformer had blown out and that we must cut down on our use of electricity or the entire camp might be in darkness for three weeks. This rumor may have been a ploy to frighten us into cutting down on our use of hot plates, but if it was, it worked. We conserved with great care what little we had of the precious resources that gave us a few creature comforts.

The shortage of barracks caused unhappiness, not only among the new arrivals, but among the groups trying to organize the camp's activities. The Education Department, for instance, wanted barracks for schools, and the Recreation Department was equally anxious to secure barracks for its projects. The Placement Bureau also had its troubles. It had begun placing residents at various jobs throughout camp, but was accused by many of favoritism and patronage, and the administration, caught in the middle, quickly became the target of everyone's ire. A call for sugar beet workers on outside farms was immediately filled, because there were any number of men who wanted to escape the confusion and disarray of life inside the barbed wire.

We took frequent trips to the Canteen, hoping to find an outside newspaper, but usually found nothing more exciting than canned carrot juice, something I had never encountered before coming to Topaz. Finally, in desperation, we subscribed to the *New York Times*.

On the advice of the government, the Canteen was one of the first enterprises to be turned over to the residents and was soon operated as a Consumers' Cooperative. From its inception, my father served as chairman of the Board of Directors and as president of the Cooperative

Congress, enabling him to keep busy and to help other people, the two essential ingredients in his life.

It wasn't long before the Coop had a paid-in resident membership capitalization of close to $5,000, and in November the Canteen grossed over $20,000. It eventually included such services as a barber shop and a radio repair shop, and in later months it opened two movie houses and a dry goods store that grossed almost $2,700 on its opening day.

As mornings and nights grew colder, we looked with increased longing at the black iron stove that stood uselessly outside our barrack waiting for work crews to bring it inside and connect it. Although we had instructions not to install the stoves ourselves, many of our neighbors had disregarded the notice and done exactly that. Such were the ways of our camp bureaucracy that our neighbors' independence secured them some heat, while our acquiescence to orders almost cost us our stove.

One day almost a month after our arrival, a work crew composed of resident men appeared, not to install our stove, but to carry it off along with others that remained outside. Fortunately, my father was home at the time and quickly pointed out the injustice of the situation. "That's not fair, is it?" he asked. "Why do you penalize only those who obeyed instructions?" The work crew knew he was right and not one man gave him an argument. They quietly carried our stove inside and installed it without further delay. At last, thanks to Papa, we had some heat in our room. Not only were we reasonably warm, there was some improvement in our food as well. The correlation between good food and rising spirits was, I discovered, pathetically simple.

By now my sister had regained her health and was busy helping to organize a nursery school system for Topaz, while I applied for work in the elementary school system. We both earned a salary of $19 a month for a forty-hour work week.

At the first meeting of the educational staff, we were addressed by Dr. John C. Carlisle, head of the Education Section, and by the assistant director of education and recreation of the War Relocation Authority. They both seemed sensitive to our special needs and presented plans for a community school with a flexible informal program appropriate to life in Topaz. There was to be no "Americanization" such as saluting the flag. A syllabus had been prepared by a Stanford University Summer Session class outlining the core curriculum we were to use, and Dr. Carlisle expressed the hope that schools could open in a few days.

The two elementary schools were to be located in Blocks 8 and 41, at the two opposite corners of camp, and the following day I went with one of the white teachers employed at Topaz to inspect Block 8. We were shocked to discover, however, that all the school barracks were absolutely bare. There were no stoves, no tables or chairs, no light bulbs, no supplies, no equipment of any kind. Nothing. The teacher invited me back to her quarters to write up our report, and I was astonished to see how comfortable a barrack could be when it was properly furnished.

The white staff members at Topaz lived in special barracks located near the Administration Building. This woman and her husband had come as teachers, bringing with them a six-month-old baby who would be cared for by a resident worker earning $16 a month. They lived in half of a barrack (the area occupied by three internee families), with linoleum and carpeting on the floor, a houseful of comfortable furniture, a fully equipped kitchen, and all the usual household objects that make up a home. Furnished in this way, their quarters didn't even look like an Army barrack. I was amazed at the transformation and realized this was the first time in six months I had been inside a normally furnished home. I was filled with envy, longing, and resentment. Until I had seen these comfortable and well-furnished quarters, I hadn't realized how much I missed our home in Berkeley, and more than anything I longed to be back once more in our house on Stuart Street.

I was assigned to register children and to teach the second grade at the school in Block 41, located at the opposite end of camp, farthest from the Administration Building. All the teachers there were resident Japanese, while the white teachers were all assigned to Block 8, close to the Administration Building and to their own home barracks. When we went to inspect the barracks of Block 41, the situation was even more alarming than was the case in Block 8. There were large holes in the roof where the stove pipes were to fit, inner sheetrock walls had not been installed, floors were covered with dust and dirt, and again there were no supplies or equipment for teaching.

It seemed useless even to attempt opening the schools, but the administrator in charge of elementary school education, an insensitive and ineffectual white man, ordered the registration for classes to proceed as scheduled on Monday, October 19. The children flocked to school in great numbers, but it was too cold to work inside the barracks, so we registered them outside at tables set up in the sun.

The following day when the children arrived, we had to send them back home because the school barracks were still unusable and we still had no supplies.

On Wednesday the barracks remained untouched, although construction of the guard towers and the barbed wire fence around the camp were proceeding without delay. When Dillon S. Myer, head of the War Relocation Authority, visited our camp, he was questioned about the need for a fence, but replied it was under the jurisdiction of the Army, which was free to do whatever it felt necessary for our protection.

It was impossible for the children to sit inside the unheated school barracks still frigid with nighttime temperatures of thirty degrees, so we tried moving our classes outside. But the feeble morning sun did little to dispel the penetrating cold, so once again, after half an hour, we sent the children home. As a solution, we switched the daily teachers' meeting to the morning and tried to hold classes in the afternoon when the barracks, though still incomplete, were at least a little warmer.

Before stoves or inner sheetrock walls were installed, we had another violent dust storm that brought to a head a long-simmering crisis in the entire school system. One day about noon, I saw gray-brown clouds massing in the sky, and a hot sultry wind seemed to signal the coming of another storm. I waited for word that schools would be closed for the afternoon, but none was forthcoming.

I dreaded the long seven-block walk to school, but shortly after lunch, I set out with a scarf wrapped around my head so it covered my nose and mouth as well. By the time I was half way to Block 41, the wind grew so intense, I felt as though I were caught in the eye of a dust hurricane. Feeling panicky, I thought of running home, but realized I was as far from my own barrack now as I was from school, and it was possible some children might be at the school.

Soon barracks only a few feet away were completely obscured by walls of dust and I was terrified the wind would knock me off my feet. Every few yards, I stopped to lean against a barrack to catch my breath, then lowering my head against the wind, I plodded on. When I got to school, I discovered many children had braved the storm as well and were waiting for me in the dust-filled classroom.

I was touched, as always, to see their eagerness to learn despite the desolation of their surroundings, the meager tools for learning, and, in this case, the physical dangers they encountered just to reach school. At the time their cheerful resiliency encouraged me, but I've wondered since if the bewildering trauma of the forced removal from their homes inflicted permanent damage to their young psyches.

Although I made an attempt to teach, so much dust was pouring into the room from all sides as well as the hole in the roof that it soon became impossible, and I decided to send the children home before the storm grew worse. "Be very careful and run home as fast as you can," I cautioned, and the other teachers of Block 41 dismissed their classes as well.

That night the wind still hadn't subsided, but my father went out to a meeting he felt he shouldn't miss. As my mother, sister, and I waited out the storm in our room, the wind reached such force we thought our barrack would be torn from its feeble foundations. Pebbles and rocks rained against the walls, and the newspapers we stuffed into the cracks in the siding came flying back into the room. The air was so thick with the smoke-like dust, my mouth was gritty with it and my lungs seemed penetrated by it. For hours the wind shrieked around our shuddering barrack, and I realized how frightened my mother was when I saw her get down on her knees to pray at her cot. I had never seen her do that before.

The wind stopped short of destroying our camp, and Papa came home safely, covered with dust, but I wondered what I would do if I had a roomful of children under my care during another such storm. The sobering reality was that I could do nothing. Although our barrack had held, I learned later that many of the camp's chicken coops had been blown out into the desert.

The following day the head of the elementary schools reprimanded us for having dismissed school without his permission.

"But we have no telephones in the barracks," we pointed out to him. "How could we have reached you at the Administration Building at the opposite end of camp?"

We were infuriated by him. We could put up with all the physical inadequacies, abysmal as they were, but such insensitive arrogance and officiousness from a white employee were galling, and more than we could bear. By then we were so frustrated, angry, and despondent that the teachers of Block 41 were ready to resign en masse. The high school teachers with problems of their own were similarly demoralized. We all went to Dr. Carlisle with our troubles, and because he was wise enough to respect our dignity and accord us some genuine understanding, the mass resignation of the resident teaching staff was averted. Eventually a new and able elementary school head was appointed and we tried once more to resume classes.

Someone named it
Topaz . . .
This land
Where neither grass
Nor trees
Nor wild flowers grow.

Banished to this
Desert land,
I cherish the
Blessing of the sky.

The fury of the
Dust storm spent,
I gaze through tears
At the sunset glow.

Grown old so soon
In a foreign land,
What do they think,
These people
Eating in lonely silence?

Yukari

8. Topaz: Winter's Despair

⌒⌁⌒ Toward the end of October we began to see snow on the mountains that ringed our desert and even afternoons began to grow cold. A coal shortage soon developed and hot water was limited to the two hours between 7:00 and 9:00 P.M., bringing on a hectic scramble for the showers each evening.

The sheetrock crews finally came to our block, but moved so slowly that they still had not reached our barrack when the first snows fell on Topaz. As though to compensate for this delay, small ten by twenty inch mirrors were installed over each basin in the washroom. But by this time, I had grown so accustomed to washing my face without a mirror, I found it rather disturbing to look up and see my strange sun-browned face looking back at me.

On October 30, over a month after our arrival, the sheetrock crew finally reached our room. "Hurray! About time! We've been waiting for you!" We greeted them with much enthusiasm, only to learn that as of the previous day they had been given orders to install ceilings only. It was a bitter disappointment, but a ceiling was better than nothing, and we quickly carried our belongings next door while the sheetrock crew worked on our room. The new ceiling made the room cozier, and sounds from the neighboring rooms were now muffled, much to our mutual relief.

A week later, with no explanation at all, another work crew appeared to install our sheetrock walls. We didn't ask any questions. We were by now prepared for any kind of irrational behavior from those in charge of our lives, and we simply carried all our possessions once more to our neighbors' room, while the new crew put up our sheet-rock walls. We now had our stove and we had our walls. My father was anxious to put up some shelves so we could make our room more comfortable, and we looked forward to being able to settle down at last.

My mother immediately ordered some heavy monk's cloth to make curtains separating our cots from the general "living area" near the stove. We needed this visual separation badly to give us a little privacy when one of us was ill or when someone came to talk Coop business with my father when the rest of us wanted to relax.

Our friends continued to stop by in Topaz as they had in Tanforan, and we all gathered around the table near the stove where a kettle of hot water was always on hand for tea. Some were young people who came to see my sister and me, while others were Issei friends of my parents. Sometimes the gatherings were lighthearted, but sometimes they were somber and sad. Once an elderly Issei friend wept as he said to my father, "Uchida San, I'm old and I may die before the war ends. I don't want to die and be buried in a place like this."

Because our family had always been close, it wasn't too difficult for us to adjust to living at such close quarters. For other families, however, the tensions of one-room living proved more destructive. Many children drifted away from their parents, rarely bothering to spend time in their own barracks, even eating all their meals with friends at other mess halls. The concept of family was rapidly breaking down, adding to the growing misery of life in camp.

Our friends on the outside continued to help make our lives bearable with their many letters and packages. My mother's former teacher, still a cherished friend, now returned in kind the love my mother had given her as a young, admiring student. She wrote us often, and for my November birthday she sent a carton containing homemade cupcakes, candles, and two jars of chocolate frosting, all securely tied down so everything arrived in perfect condition. For my gift she sent an heirloom silver teaspoon that once belonged to her grandmother, and knowing how much my mother missed flowers, she also included a bouquet of flowers, each stem wrapped carefully in wet cotton. Throughout the war, white friends such as these supported and sustained us, and their letters followed us as we moved from camp to cities in the east and eventually back to California.

Other Japanese, however, were not so fortunate in their friends. There were some farmers who entrusted their farms to white contractors and trustees, only to be systematically robbed of enormous wartime profits during their absence. Others who had given "power of attorney" to white "friends" also lost possessions that were sold without their knowledge.

A succession of dust storms, rain squalls, and a severe snowstorm finally brought our limping schools to a complete halt in mid-November. The snowfall was beautiful, obliterating the ugliness of our camp with its pristine white, but within an hour the roads were trampled with footprints and the few perfect moments were gone. Snow blew in from the holes still remaining in our roof and it was impossible to endure the ten degree Fahrenheit temperatures even though we were bundled up in coats, scarves, and boots. My fingers and toes often ached from the cold.

Finally it was officially announced that schools would close and not reopen until they were fully winterized with sheetrock walls and stoves. It was close to miraculous that we had been able to hold classes for as long as we had, and it was only because the children were so eager to come and the parents so anxious to have some order in their lives.

My class had just begun a Thanksgiving project of cardboard cabins and pilgrims, and the children were reluctant to leave it half-completed.

"Never mind," I told them. "It'll keep. And when we get back, our rooms will be warm. Won't that be wonderful?"

The children agreed, but I think some of them would have been willing to endure the cold to keep coming to school, for there was little else in Topaz for them to do. Despite our limitations, we had had some good times together. We once got permission to go outside the gates to visit a nearby sheepherder; we had a pet fish in a glass jar whose death we mourned with a funeral; one day we experienced the excitement of finding a snake in our classroom; and we had small parties for holidays and birthdays. But most important, the children had some sense of purpose in their lives as long as they were coming to school to learn.

With the approach of the holiday season, a few rather touching attempts were made to bring some cheer into our drab lives. One afternoon the high school band from Delta came in their fine red uniforms to give us a concert. They played to a full house of appreciative residents, and the following week a group of entertainers from Topaz went to Delta in exchange.

Through the determined efforts of the residents, our first Thanksgiving in camp was a relatively happy occasion. The men of our block had spent the entire day planting willow saplings that had been transported into camp from somewhere beyond the desert. The young trees looked too frail to survive in the alkaline soil, but we all felt anything was worth trying. We longed desperately for something green, some trees or shrubs or plants so we might have something to look forward to with the approach of spring. There existed a master plan that called for the planting of one large tree in front of every mess hall and the lining of the two-hundred-foot-wide firebreaks between each block with trees as well. It was a nice thought, and efforts to make it a reality got under way in December, but were eventually defeated by the harsh climate and the unfriendly soil. Our desert remained a desert, and not even the industrious Japanese Americans could transform it into anything else.

During November, for some unexplained reason known only to the Army, many people who had property stored in government warehouses suddenly had their belongings shipped out to them in the desert. We wondered if the Army was trying to tell us we could never return to California and that it wanted to be rid of our possessions as well as our presence.

At any rate, this enabled some residents to wear clothing they hadn't expected to use in camp. For our Thanksgiving dinner we all put aside our slacks and bulky jackets and dug into our suitcases for our good clothes. My sister and I wore dresses and heels for the first time since coming to Topaz, Mama put on her Sunday clothes, and Papa wore his white shirt, black bow tie, and good suit. Even the cook wore a dark suit and tie.

Our mess hall was decorated with streamers and a large sign reading, "Thanksgiving Greetings from Your Mess 7 Crew." Instead of standing in line for our food as we usually did, we all sat down together and observed a moment of prayer. We were served a turkey dinner with the usual accompaniments, and to celebrate the completion of the sheetrocking of our block, we all chipped in for ice cream that was served with our pumpkin pie and coffee.

It was a dinner vastly different from our plain daily fare, and it satisfied more than our physical hunger. We were pleasantly surprised to find several talented residents in our block who entertained us with musical numbers. My father, always happy to perform, sang his "Song of Topaz" adapted from the "Missoula Camp Song" which he had written in Montana. By now it had acquired some fame among the Issei, and they loved to hear it. When the entertainment was over, we walked back to our barrack feeling a warmth and sense of community we had not known since coming to Topaz.

Occasionally we had our own private celebrations as well, such as my parents' twenty-sixth wedding anniversary. My sister and I were anxious to make this anniversary a special occasion since they had been separated on their twenty-fifth, and the limitations of our environment caused us to be imaginative. We made a scrapbook for them with photos cut from magazines of all the things we wished we could give them. There were pictures of a large baked ham, fresh fruits, bowls and bowls of fresh vegetables and salads, and an array of fancy desserts. We also included pictures of such gifts as crystals and a silver tea service. What we actually served at a tea for their friends were tuna sandwiches, cookies, and ice cream from the Canteen, but Mama and Papa seemed genuinely touched and pleased by our simple childlike efforts.

Sometime in December, when stoves and sheetrock walls were finally installed, schools were able to reopen at last, this time for all-day sessions. It was a great relief to be warm in my classroom, and the atmosphere was further improved by bright colored curtains my mother had sewn for me by hand. Life settled down at last to a fairly stable routine, and this now included a weekly headcount of all residents every Monday evening.

Increasing numbers of outside visitors came to observe conditions in our camp, and one of them was the director of the International House at the University of California in Berkeley. A group of former students and alumni gathered to hear him speak, as he told of the changes the war had brought to Berkeley—the blackouts, the food shortages, and the flood of defense workers into the city. We were saddened and frustrated to realize that when manpower was so badly needed in America's war effort, we Japanese Americans were not only denied the right to serve our country, but had been made its unwilling victims.

Among our visitors was Margaret G. Bondfield, a former British minister of labor who had served four times in Parliament. My parents were invited to a dinner in her honor at the home of an administrative officer, and my sister and I were able to meet her at a breakfast meeting. I found her to be a warm individual who seemed genuinely concerned about our plight, and I invited her to visit my class the next day. The children were thrilled to have her sign our guest book and to see the string of titles that followed her name. On another occasion, Governor and Mrs. Maw of Utah came to visit Topaz and were invited to participate in ceremonies to install our City Council.

Some visitors were from church groups and came to provide spiritual comfort as well as to observe conditions in our camp. They occupied the pulpits of our churches, and their words often gave a temporary lift to the monotony of our days.

Other visitors came not to provide solace, but to investigate whether the taxpayers' money was being misused. One day I was startled to have the chairman of the City Council, several camp dignitaries, including my father, and five senators from the Utah State Legislature walk into my classroom while observing our school. The senators had come to tour Topaz to see for themselves whether we were being coddled, as had been reported in their newspapers. Although they came after winterization of the barracks had been completed, I doubt whether they found we were being pampered. We were subject to the same rationing restrictions that applied to civilians outside, and our food budget was approximately 39 cents per person, per day. This later dropped to 31 cents with stringent restrictions placed on coffee and milk.

Representatives of the National Japanese American Student Relocation Council also came in to talk to students interested in leaving camp, and worked diligently to help them further their education. I had passed up an earlier opportunity to go to Smith College from Tanforan because I felt I should stay with my fellow internees and make some positive contribution to our situation. Now, however, I longed to get out of this dreary camp, return to civilization, and continue my education. I applied for enrollment in the Education Department at Smith College in Northampton, Massachusetts, but discovered the earlier opening there was no longer available. I also discovered that the process for obtaining a leave clearance was long and tedious. One did not decide to leave and simply walk out the gates. I waited impatiently and with increasing frustration as the weeks passed.

The policy of the War Relocation Authority was to encourage early depopulation of the camps, and qualified citizens were permitted to leave as early as July 1942. Permission was granted if (a) the applicant had a place to go and means of supporting himself or herself; (b) FBI and intelligence records showed that the applicant would not endanger national security; (c) there was no evidence that his or her presence in a community would cause a public disturbance; and (d) the applicant agreed to keep the War Relocation Authority informed of his or her address at all times. In October, aliens who met the above qualifications were also permitted to leave.

Students were among the first internees to leave the camps, and others followed to midwestern and eastern cities where previously few Japanese Americans had lived. Government procedures for clearing colleges as well as students were so slow, however, that in March of 1943 there was still a logjam in Washington of three hundred requests for leave clearance. The National Japanese American Student Relocation Council eventually assisted some three thousand students to leave the camps and enter over five hundred institutions of higher learning throughout the country.

As Christmas approached, the days grew sharp and brittle with cold. Morning temperatures hovered close to zero, and the ice-covered saplings looked like fragile crystal ornaments glistening at the edge of the firebreaks. We decorated small greasewood Christmas trees in our classrooms and held an Open House for the parents at our schools. I gave my children a party with apples and milk from the mess hall, and the two elementary schools tried to present a joint Christmas program at Block 1. But inadequate planning, a shortage of chairs, and the lack of a public address system combined to produce a near riot among the over-stimulated, excited children. I was greatly relieved when we adjourned early and sent the children home for Christmas recess.

A special Christmas tea was held at the art school, and my parents were among the hosts and hostesses as they were at many of the camp's social functions. I decided to stop by for a look, but left quickly when I discovered that all the women were in dresses and high heels and that my baggy slacks were very much out of place amid the rather formal festivities.

The residents tried whenever they could to re-create some of the more gracious moments of their former lives, and a Christmas tea, even though held in a dusty barrack in the middle of a bleak desert, gave some small sense of dignity to the demeaned lives they now led.

On Christmas Eve, carolers from church came to our barrack to sing for us, and from early morning on Christmas day friends came from all parts of the vast camp to call on us. Christmas was a day for friends, and even in camp our family was fortunate to have them in abundance. It wasn't until afternoon that we were able to make some calls of our own, taking with us some of the evergreen sprays shipped to us from my mother's friends in Cornwall, Connecticut.

"*Ah, ureshii.* I'm so happy," Mama had said, burying her face in the fragrant branches when they arrived, and she couldn't rest until she had shared them with those of our friends who were too old or ill to come visit us. She kept only a few branches for herself, taking the rest to more than ten families.

Gifts had come into Topaz and to other camps from all over the United States, many collected by church groups and the American Friends Service Committee, which sent out a plea for 50,000 Christmas gifts for the internees. In many cases correspondences and friendships developed that lasted long after the war ended, and we were touched by the compassion and concern some Americans felt for us.

After making our Christmas calls, the four of us went together to our church service, and by the time we walked home, it was growing dark and the wind was piercing cold. We had a pleasant dinner at the mess hall and settled down to a quiet evening beside our glowing stove. It wasn't often that our family had an evening just to ourselves, and it was a pleasant change.

As the year drew to a close, my sister and I redoubled our efforts to leave Topaz. I couldn't face the thought of beginning another year without some hope of leaving, for by now many of my friends had gone out to schools throughout the United States. Those of us who remained in camp did our best to make life pleasant and productive, but it was mostly a time of suspended expectations. I worked hard to be a good teacher; I went to meetings, wrote long letters to my friends, knitted sweaters and socks, devoured any books I could find, listened to the radio, went to art school and to church and to lectures by outside visitors. I spent time socializing with friends and I saw an occasional movie at the Coop. I also had a wisdom tooth removed at the hospital and suffered a swollen face for three days. I caught one cold after another; I fell on the unpaved roads; I lost my voice from the dust; I got homesick and angry and despondent. And sometimes I cried.

No matter what I did, I was still in an artificial government-spawned community on the periphery of the real world. I was in a dismal, dreary camp surrounded by barbed wire in the middle of a stark, harsh landscape that offered nothing to refresh the eye or heal the spirit.

I wrote dozens of letters to the National Japanese American Student Relocation Council (whose staff by now seemed like friends) and filled out countless forms, determined to go anywhere if the fellowship to Smith College failed to materialize. My sister also filled out numerous applications, hoping to find an opening in her line of work.

Even a brief exit from the gates was remarkably refreshing. From time to time residents were given special permits to go out to nearby Delta or Fillmore on official business. One day our elementary school supervisor took five of us teachers to visit one of Delta's elementary schools. We visited the first, second, and third grades where, for the first time in many months, I saw blond and brown-haired children. I marveled at the skill of the professional teacher and went back to camp determined to improve my own teaching methods. But the delicious lunch at the Southern Hotel and the ice cream soda later in the day were just as important to me as the visit to the school, and lingered as a pleasant memory for several days.

Another day my sister and I got permission to go to Delta with a white staff member to buy supplies for the nursery school. We had only a half hour in which to race from one store to another, but the joy of being in a real town and shopping freely in the outside world was a tremendous tonic to our spirits. These brief glimpses of life on the outside not only cheered us, but also increased our appetite for a permanent return to its freedom.

My father, as a judicial commissioner, was also able on one occasion to go out to Fillmore on business with some officials. He didn't return until 9:30 that night, but walked into our room looking absolutely rejuvenated, and laden with the makings of a fine late night snack. Besides fruit, cookies, and candy, he had purchased butter (57 cents a pound), eggs (50 cents a dozen), bacon (47 cents a pound) and cups and saucers (35 cents each). It had been over a year since he had walked freely along the streets of a city, able to enter any shop, buy whatever he pleased, and bring home treats for the family as he used to do.

He also brought home an interesting tale that gave us a good laugh. He told how, at the gate, the driver had reported to the guard, "There are six of us including Caucasians," whereupon the guard peered into the car asking, "Which one of you is Mr. Caucasians?" It seemed that some who patrolled our boundaries and were in charge of our security were not very literate men.

After considerable thought, my parents decided to apply for permission to visit my aging grandmother who had been sent to the Heart Mountain Relocation Center in Wyoming with my aunt and uncle's family. It required weeks of paperwork and many teletypes to Washington before my father, an "enemy alien on parole," was able to secure permission to travel from one government camp to another, accompanied by my "enemy alien" mother. They started out on their camp-to-camp journey one morning, and as soon as they reached Delta they bought two dozen oranges and assorted groceries which they sent back to my sister and me via their car driver. During their ten-day trip they continued to send us postcards and letters all along the way, linking us as closely as possible with their own pleasure in being free.

It cheered my father enormously to see his mother and sister for the first time since the war broke out. But more than that, it was the trip itself, enabling my parents to live freely outside the barbed wire enclosure even for a brief period, that had renewed their spirits. When they returned, they had an entirely different air about them. My mother looked so pretty and buoyant, and they both seemed refreshed and rejuvenated. It was good to have them back, but it seemed a pity that they had to immerse themselves once more in the barren life at Topaz.

As time went on, the residents of Topaz began to release their frustrations on each other in acts that seemed foreign to the Japanese nature. In communities where they had lived prior to the war, most of them had been respectable, hardworking people. There was, of course, the usual percentage of the dishonest and disreputable who inhabit any community, but the corrosive nature of life in camp seemed to bring out the worst in many people, provoking them into doing things they probably would not have done outside. There was shoplifting in the dry goods store and false receipts were turned in for rebate at the Canteen. On the outside, such crimes were extremely rare among Japanese Americans in those days. One of our neighbors narrowly escaped being attacked as she crossed the high school lot one night, and women no longer felt safe walking alone after dark.

My father was increasingly harassed by people who felt the Coop was not being properly administered, and these malcontents often brought their grievances to our room. My mother, sister, and I spent many tense evenings behind our monk's cloth barrier, listening to hostile and abusive remarks shouted at my father.

One night I was finally so provoked by these crude men and their vilifications that I emulated the artist at Tanforan and put up a big "Quarantined" sign on our door. But the next morning neighbors and friends came knocking on our door to inquire who was sick and what was wrong, so my father, embarrassed, quickly took down the sign. It was hopeless. There was no escape.

Other camps seemed to have had more internal friction and violence than Topaz, but we had our share of it. Issei and Nisei resident leaders met often trying to arbitrate the differences among various factions in camp, and my father would sometimes be out until 2:00 and 3:00 A.M. attending such meetings.

Dillon S. Myer, director of the War Relocation Authority camps, later wrote about what being cut off from the mainstream of American life can do to people. "It saps the initiative, weakens the instincts of human dignity and freedom, creates doubts, misgivings and tensions."[1] He went on to describe how the Japanese Americans, once so enterprising and energetic, had grown increasingly obsessed with feelings of helplessness, personal insecurity, and inertia the longer they remained in camp.

Such feelings were overtaking me as well and increased my desperation to get out of camp. Internal squabbling spread like a disease. Even the resident doctors at the hospital had their difficulties, requiring the mediation of a special committee. Much of the friction arose simply because the doctors were overworked. My mother once went to the hospital hoping to be examined for a lingering cough, but after waiting for several hours, came home unattended. "No one had time to see me. The doctors are all too busy," she said, and she never went back. Neither could she bring herself to go to the hospital to have a wart removed from her cheek. When it first appeared shortly after the outbreak of war, she had said it was just one of her tears, dried on her face. In camp it seemed to be growing and we urged her to have it removed. But she wouldn't do it. "I can't bother those busy doctors with such a small thing," she said. "Maybe it will go away when peace comes."

People crowded the hospital with all manner of minor ailments, but there were others who had such serious illnesses as tuberculosis, pneumonia, and kidney disease. There were residents who needed major surgery, there were pregnant women who required prenatal care, there were births, and there were deaths. Life went on, even though in many ways it was standing still for us.

One woman, whose husband was imprisoned early and interned in

1. Dillon S. Myer, "The WRA Says Thirty," *The New Republic* 112 (June 25, 1945): 867–68.

Louisiana, died suddenly following surgery. Her husband was permitted to come to Topaz for her funeral, but only under escort by two armed guards. Upon his arrival he was placed, not in a situation that might have given him some solace, but in the camp guardhouse. Outraged community welfare workers demanded his immediate release, and he was permitted to remain in a barrack, but his guards were stationed in the adjoining room. He was allowed to stay in Topaz only long enough to attend the funeral, with no time to mourn his loss in the comforting presence of his friends, and was promptly sent back to his Louisiana internment camp.

One of the funerals I attended in camp was for the father of a friend of mine. She had returned from school in Colorado for the occasion, and it must have been devastating for her to see the bleakness of Topaz for the first time, knowing her father had spent his last days in such a place. The funeral service was brief, and his coffin was decorated with cascades of crepe paper flowers painstakingly made by some Issei women. Many of those who died in Topaz were buried in the desert, and it seemed a bitter irony that only then were they outside the barbed wire fence.

In mid-January the Spanish consul arrived on behalf of the Japanese government to investigate the treatment accorded Japanese nationals in camp. Prior to his arrival, a group of Issei, including my father, held many meetings to determine the grievances to be placed before the visiting diplomat.

One of our Issei friends spoke to me about the matter one day saying, "It's too bad you Nisei have no country to take your grievances to, Yoshiko San, since it's your own country that's put you behind barbed wire." He was, of course, absolutely right, and I could only agree with him.

At the time, our former home state, far from being concerned about our welfare, had lost none of its vituperative hatred for us. We heard there were still racist groups in California who wanted to revoke the citizenship of all Japanese Americans, exclude us permanently from the state, and repatriate us to Japan at the end of the war. If our home state didn't want us back, I wondered, where would we go at the end of the war?

On January 28, 1943, Secretary of War Stimson announced a complete reversal of Army policy. Until that time, since June of 1942, all Nisei men had been classified IV-C (not acceptable for service because of ancestry) and had not been inducted by the Selective Service, nor accepted when they volunteered. Now the secretary of war stated that the Army had decided to accept Nisei and, furthermore, that it wanted to create a special all-Nisei combat team. In February the Army began a recruitment program for this project, seeking volunteers from all the camps.

In the same month, President Roosevelt made a statement issued, it seemed, a year too late:

> No loyal citizen of the United States should be denied the democratic right to exercise the responsibilities of his citizenship, regardless of his ancestry.
>
> The principle on which this country was founded and by which it has always governed is that Americanism is a matter of the mind and heart.
>
> Americanism is not, and never was, a matter of race or ancestry.
>
> Every loyal American citizen should be given the opportunity to serve this country wherever his skills will make the greatest contribution— whether it be in the ranks of our armed forces, war production, agriculture, Government service, or other work essential to the war effort.

Recruiters from the War Department were sent to all the camps to present their case and to answer questions the residents might have. A mass meeting for this purpose took place in Topaz in early February at one of the camp's central mess halls, and an overflow crowd attended.

The recruiters maintained that if the Nisei were diffused throughout the Army they would simply be additional manpower and nothing more. As an all-Nisei combat team, they pointed out, their actions would gain special attention, allowing the Nisei to prove their loyalty in a dramatic, forceful way to the entire country.

But the thought of a segregated unit was abhorrent. Why, we wondered, couldn't the Nisei simply serve as other Americans? Why should they be singled out when it hadn't been deemed necessary to create an all-Italian or an all-German unit? Wouldn't a segregated unit simply invite further discrimination and perhaps simplify their deployment to the most dangerous combat zones? These were urgent questions asked by the Nisei as well as the Issei of Topaz.

Some Issei were outspoken about their disdain for such a plan. They asked why the Nisei should volunteer to fight for a country that had deprived them of every right as citizens and placed them behind barbed wire. They wondered why the Nisei should now offer their lives for a country that still did not accept them as it did other Americans and wanted to place them in segregated units.

Many of the Nisei men in camp were of draft age. Rejected and incarcerated by their own country, they were now being asked to show their loyalty to that same country by volunteering. They were told by the recruiters that the future of the Nisei in America might well be determined by their decision.

The presence of the Army recruiters caused tremendous turmoil in our camp. As part of their recruiting process the Army required a mass registration of all draft age Nisei men. The situation was complicated by a simultaneous War Relocation Authority mass registration for all other Nisei and Issei residents in connection with leave clearance and release from the camps. The timing, coinciding as it did with the Army recruitment, could not have been worse.

Question 28 in both Army and War Relocation Authority forms contained the question: "Will you swear unqualified allegiance to the United States of America and forswear any form of allegiance or obedience to the Japanese Emperor, or any other foreign government power or organization?" It was an inept and foolish attempt to determine the respondent's loyalty.

Since, at the time, the Issei were by law classified "aliens ineligible for citizenship," acquiescence to Question 28 would have left them without a country. The ill-conceived question was eventually revised in a manner acceptable to the Issei, but only after it caused untold confusion, alarm, and unnecessary anguish.

For the Nisei men Question 28 was equally unacceptable, for it was a loaded question that implied a nonexistent allegiance to the Emperor of Japan. The Army's Question 27 was also a problem for them. It asked, "Are you willing to serve in the armed forces of the United States on combat duty, wherever ordered?" Many Nisei men felt they could not answer yes to that question until their civil rights were restored, and only with the proviso that they not be placed in a segregated unit. Unable to qualify their answers in this way, they could only answer no to Question 27 as well as 28. The men who answered no to both questions were sometimes referred to as the "no-no boys."

There were some Nisei men, however, who answered yes to both questions and volunteered for the all-Nisei combat team. Some volunteered because they felt it was the only way to prove the loyalty of the Nisei to the United States. Others went because they were as eager to fight fascism as any other American.

The Nisei men of draft age were asked to make an agonizing decision inside the concentration camps of America. There were those critical of the "no-no" men and there were those critical of the men who answered yes and volunteered. I believe it required uncommon courage to make either decision under intolerable circumstances.

One Nisei who volunteered from Topaz was a father past draft age. He did so, he said, because he believed the future of the Nisei was indeed at stake and he wanted to set an example for the younger men.

A few of my friends volunteered from Topaz, as did two eighteen-year-old boys from our Japanese church in Oakland. My sister had taught both of them in her Sunday School class, and they came to say goodbye to us before they left camp. Some of my former college classmates also volunteered from other camps, and two of them never came back.

The magnificent record of the 442nd Regimental Combat Team and the 100th Infantry Battalion, composed of Japanese Americans from Hawaii as well as the continental United States, is now well known, and serves as a testament to the extraordinary bravery of some fine Nisei men.

As spring made its way to our desert camp, there was only a slight touch of warmth in the air. Everywhere I looked, there was only the hard white glare of bleached sand and no sign of the renewal of life so abundant in California. I would have been glad to see even the disdained dandelions my father used to dig out in such numbers from our lawn.

We nurtured carefully a single daffodil bulb a friend had sent us, planting it in an old tin can and watching it closely each day. When that golden flower finally burst open, it was an occasion of real rejoicing, and I was amazed at the pleasure even a single flower could bring.

One morning when I opened our door, I saw a flock of seagulls winging westward in the desert sky. "Come look! Hurry!" I shouted to everybody. I didn't know where they had come from or where they were going, but their shrill cries brought back with painful clarity the sounds of San Francisco Bay. For a fleeting moment I was touched by the beauty and grace of their soaring flight, and overwhelmed with thoughts of home.

Most of the saplings, planted so hopefully in the fall, had died because nothing nourished their fragile roots, and the children finished what the hostile soil began by playing leapfrog over the dying trees as they walked to and from school. Even the large tree in front of our mess hall remained only a dark skeleton despite the encouragement and tender care it received from the residents.

Although there were many such discouraging setbacks, the people of Topaz never gave up in their efforts to improve the camp. One day all the able-bodied men of our block went out on trucks to a distant river bed to collect gravel to pave the roads. The gravel, it was hoped, might hold down the dust and prevent the roads from becoming mired in mud during rainstorms.

My father was older than the other men who volunteered, but he insisted on going with them. We had tried before to dissuade him from taking on so many extra functions, from making the announcements at our mess hall to presiding at block parties and wedding receptions. He and my mother also served as "go-betweens" for many young couples. "You just try to do too much, Papa," we would tell him. But he continued to ignore what I suppose to him were bothersome concerns, and did exactly as he pleased. He was gone for most of the day and came home with a terrible sunburn and blisters on both hands, but that night he went to church to speak at a young people's meeting.

Occasionally, groups were permitted to go to the nearby mountains in trucks for rock-hunting parties, but it wasn't always necessary to go beyond the gates. With luck, we sometimes found old arrowheads, trilobites, or unusual stones inside the camp grounds, and we often walked head down, eyes on the ground, in search of some small hidden treasure.

A group of internees at Topaz taking a break from digging a ditch for a Coop
water pipe. *Courtesy of Mr. and Mrs. Emil Sekerak*

One evening a sixty-three-year-old man, probably absorbed in such a search, was shot to death by an MP on duty in one of the guard towers. The guard claimed he had shouted four times for the man to halt, but that the man had tried to crawl out under the fence. His body, however, was found more than three feet inside the fence and he probably hadn't heard the guard's calls from the high tower several hundred feet away.

The death caused an uproar throughout camp. Everyone was outraged that the MP had not fired a warning shot before aiming to kill. How far, after all, could the man have gone, even if he had crawled under the fence. If it happened once, the residents reasoned, it could happen again. And what about the safety of the children? Block meetings were held, investigations got under way, and the Spanish consul arrived once more in great haste. A week later, the furor still hadn't abated. We never learned what punishment, if any, was meted out to the guard, but a campwide funeral was held for the victim, and he was laid to rest in the desert with reverberations of the event still shaking the entire camp.

Spring, instead of bringing peace to Topaz, heightened the general feeling of unrest, and a small group of pro-Japan agitators became increasingly threatening. These men, tough, arrogant, and belligerent, blatantly fashioned knives and other weapons from scrap metal and sat sharpening them in front of their barracks. Some were Issei, some were Kibei. All were angry, and focused their resentment primarily on those Issei who worked in positions of responsibility and leadership requiring close contact with the white administrative staff.

One night the head of the art school was attacked by a group of these men, and we worried about my father who often walked home alone on the dark unlit roads after meetings. We wanted him to cut down on his committee work, for now in addition to the Coop and the Judicial Commission, he was on the Arbitration Board, was chairman of the Church Finance Committee, and had been asked to run for city manager as well. Like many of the other Issei leaders, he was respected and well-liked in Topaz and soon became one of the targets of the agitators.

Two of these disgruntled men came to warn my father one night that he was being too obsequious to the white administrative staff. It was an ugly, threatening confrontation, and although my father dismissed it casually, the rest of us, including his friends, were deeply concerned for his safety. His life, it seemed, was being threatened by the very Japanese he was trying to help.

The harassment of Issei leaders increased, and one of the church ministers who also devoted much time to community service was attacked one night by three masked men wielding lead pipes. The resident internal police could do nothing to control these lawless men for their cowardly attacks always occurred late at night when the victims were alone, there were no witnesses, and they could flee undetected into the darkness.

My parents wanted to stay in camp with their friends as long as possible, but as these attacks became more frequent and violent, we urged my father to consider leaving camp too.

Good news came first for my sister. Early in May she was offered a position as assistant in the nursery school run by the education department of Mt. Holyoke College. Until she could go there in the fall, she was invited to spend the summer at Pendle Hill, Pennsylvania, a Quaker study center.

Soon thereafter, a letter came for me as well. I had been accepted at Smith College with a full graduate fellowship, covering room, board, and tuition, which had become available in the department of education. Until I could go there in the fall, I was invited to spend the summer with a family in New York City whom I had met only once when visiting Cornwall, Connecticut, as a child. The daughter, Cathy, and I had corresponded ever since that long ago meeting in Cornwall when my mother had first met her own pen pals. And now, so many years later, it was the mysterious and wonderful spinning out of the thread of friendship begun by my mother in Kyoto and catching Cathy and me in its strands that gave me a home to go to from the Utah desert.

Now there was only the wait for my indefinite leave papers, and they finally arrived on the twenty-fourth of May. Knowing how anxiously I waited for them, my father hurried down to my school with them the moment they arrived.

"Good news!" he called out, smiling and waving the papers. "Your good news has come!"

The long wait was over.

On my last day at school, the children of my class presented me with a clay bowl one of them had made, and they stood together, giggling and embarrassed, to sing one last song for me.

On our last Sunday, my sister and I went to say goodbye to all our friends, especially the older Issei who we knew would probably remain in camp until the end of the war.

It was hard for us to go, leaving behind our Issei parents in the desolation of that desert camp. And I imagine other Nisei felt as we did as they ventured forth into the outside world.

Because we Nisei were still relatively young at the time, it was largely the Issei who had led the way, guiding us through the devastation and trauma of our forced removal. When they were uprooted from their homes, many had just reached a point of financial security in their lives. During the war, however, they all suffered enormous losses, both tangible and intangible. The evacuation was the ultimate of the incalculable hardships and indignities they had borne over the years.

And yet most of our parents had continued to be steadfast and strong in spirit. Our mothers had made homes of the bleak barrack rooms, just as my own mother, in her gentle, nurturing way, had been a loving focal point for our family and friends.

Deprived of so much themselves, the Issei wanted the best for their Nisei children. Many had sacrificed to send their children to college, and they encouraged them now to leave camp to continue their education.

As my sister and I prepared for our departure, thoughts of gratitude toward our Issei parents still lay unspoken deep within us, and it was only in later years that we came to realize how much they had done for us; how much they had given us to enrich and strengthen our lives.

When we left Topaz, we didn't know that a stink bomb would be thrown into my parents' room and that the administration would clear the way for my father's release to Salt Lake City because it was too dangerous for him to stay in Topaz. We were spared that terror and

My sister (far right) and I, with our parents, on the day of our departure for the outside world. Topaz, 1943.

were able to share instead their sense of joy and release when they too were finally free.

Wearing a suit my mother had made for me, shoes ordered by mail, and a hat that came out of one of our trunks, I was ready at last to face New York City and the world outside. And I was glad to have my sister at my side to share with me whatever lay ahead beyond the barbed wire.

Some of our friends came with my mother and father to the gate to see us off, but the joy of our impending freedom was greatly tempered by the pain of leaving them behind. As I hugged my mother and father and each of my friends, I cried for them, because they could not come with us, and I cried for myself, for the sense of loss and separation that was filling my heart.

As we climbed onto the dusty bus for Delta where we would catch our train to the east, the afternoon sun was already hot and a slight breeze filled the air with a fine haze of dust. We leaned close to the window, waving bravely, wondering when we would see our parents and friends again.

And then it was time to go; the bus gave a jolt, and started down the rough unpaved road. I watched from the window as long as I could, waving until my mother and father were two small blurs in the cluster by the gate. I knew they were waving long after they could no longer see us, and I turned then to face the road ahead.

For my sister and me, the cold dark winter had come to an end, and now at last we were within reach of spring. Our long desert exile was over. We were on our way back, at last, to the world we had left over a year ago.

The budding plum
Holds my own joy
At the melting ice
And the long winter's end.

The Creator's
Blessings overflow,
And even the single lily
Has its soul.

Like the sound
Of a koto *on a*
Quiet rainy day,
So, too, this small flower
Brings solace to my heart.

Yukari

Epilogue

〰️ Our wartime evacuation is now history and has been judged one of the most shameful episodes of our country's past—indeed, one of its most egregious mistakes. The ultimate tragedy of that mistake, I believe, was that our government betrayed not only the Japanese people but all Americans, for in its flagrant violation of our Constitution, it damaged the essence of the democratic beliefs on which this country was founded. The passage of time and the emergence of heretofore unpublished documents have revealed to us today the magnitude and scope of that betrayal.

In recent years, at the urging of Japanese American leaders, this country has belatedly tried to make some amends. In 1976 President Gerald R. Ford signed a proclamation regarding Executive Order 9066 that stated in part, "not only was that evacuation wrong, but Japanese Americans were and are loyal Americans . . . we have learned from the tragedy of that long-ago experience forever to treasure liberty and justice for each individual American, and resolve that this kind of action shall never again be repeated."

As the result of diligent efforts by the Japanese American Citizens League on the issue of redress, a Commission on Wartime Relocation and Internment of Civilians was created by President Jimmy Carter and the Congress of the United States. It began its inquiry in the summer of 1981, and conducted a series of regional hearings to record the testimony of hundreds of Japanese Americans who had been interned during World War II, and of other witnesses associated with that incarceration. The commission's task is to compile an accurate official record of the wartime incarceration of the Japanese Americans and to address itself to the vital question of redress. Unfortunately, however, for many Japanese Americans it is too late. Most of the Issei who endured the hardships of our forced removal are, like my own parents, gone.

Today many of the Nisei, having overcome the traumatizing effects of their incarceration and participated in a wide spectrum of American life with no little success, are approaching retirement. Their Sansei children, who experienced the Vietnam War with its violent confrontations and protest marches, have asked questions about those early World War II years.

"Why did you let it happen?" they ask of the evacuation. "Why didn't you fight for your civil rights? Why did you go without protest to the concentration camps?"

They were right to ask these questions, for they made us search for some obscured truths and come to a better understanding of ourselves and of those times. They are the generation for whom civil rights meant more than just words. They are the generation who taught us to celebrate our ethnicity and discover our ethnic pride. Their compassion and concern for the aging Issei resulted in many worthwhile programs for all Japanese Americans.

It is my generation, however, who lived through the evacuation of 1942. We are their link to the past and we must provide them with the cultural memory they lack. We must tell them all we can remember, so they can better understand the history of their own people. As they listen to our voices from the past, however, I ask that they remember they are listening in a totally different time; in a totally changed world.

In 1942 the word "ethnic" was yet unknown and ethnic consciousness not yet awakened. There had been no freedom marches, and the voice of Martin Luther King had not been heard. The majority of the American people, supporting their country in a war they considered just, refused to acknowledge the fact that their country was denying the civil rights of fellow Americans. They would not have supported any resistance to our forced removal had it arisen, and indeed such resistance might well have been met with violence as treasonous.

Today the "relocation centers" are properly called concentration camps. The term is used not to imply any similarity to the Nazi death camps, but to indicate the true nature of the so-called "relocation centers." *Webster's New Collegiate Dictionary* defines "concentration camp" as a place in which "prisoners of war, political prisoners, foreign nationals, refugees, and the like, are confined." In our case, this definition should include citizens of the incarcerating government as well.

Today I would not allow my civil rights to be denied without strong protest, and I believe there would be many other Americans willing to stand beside me in protest.

A Japanese American recently asked me how the fourth generation Japanese Americans could be proud of their heritage when their grandparents and great grandparents had been incarcerated in concentration camps. I was stunned by the question, for quite the contrary, I think they should be proud of the way in which their grandparents survived that shattering ordeal. It is our country that should be ashamed of what it did, not the Japanese Americans for having been its victims.

Although some Issei were shattered and broken by the experience, those I knew and observed personally, endured the hardship of the evacuation with dignity, stoic composure, disciplined patience, and an amazing resiliency of spirit. I think they displayed a level of strength, grace, and courage that is truly remarkable.

Like many other Issei, my parents made the best of an intolerable situation. Throughout their internment they maintained the values and faith that sustained them all their lives. They continued to be the productive, caring human beings they had always been, and they continued always to have hope in the future. They helped my sister and me channel our anger and frustration into an effort to get out of camp and get on with our education and our lives. They didn't want us to lose our sense of purpose, and I am grateful they didn't nurture in us the kind of soul-decaying bitterness that would have robbed us of energy and destroyed us as human beings. Our anger was cathartic, but bitterness would have been self-destructive.

Perhaps I survived the uprooting and incarceration because my Issei parents taught me to endure. Perhaps I survived because at the time I believed I was taking the only viable path and believed what I was doing was right. Looking back now, I think the survival of the Japanese through those tragic, heartbreaking days was a triumph of the human spirit. And I hope future generations of Japanese Americans, remembering that, will never feel stigmatized by the incarceration of the Issei and Nisei.

From the concentration camps the Nisei went out to all parts of the United States, some to schools and others to seek employment. They were accepted with warmth and concern by some Americans, but treated with contempt and hatred by others.

The white friends to whom I went from Topaz accepted me without hesitation into the warmth of their family circle. But there were others, such as the conductor on the train I rode to Northampton, Massachusetts. "You'd better not be a Jap," he threatened as he took my ticket, "because if you are, I'll throw you off the train."

I left Topaz determined to work hard and prove I was as loyal as any other American. I felt a tremendous sense of responsibility to make good, not just for myself, but for all Japanese Americans. I felt I was representing all the Nisei, and it was sometimes an awesome burden to bear.

When the war was over, the brilliant record of the highly decorated Nisei combat teams, and favorable comments of the GIs returning from Japan, helped alleviate to some degree the hatred directed against the Japanese Americans during the war. Although racism had by no means been eliminated, new fields of employment, previously closed, gradually opened up for many Nisei. In time they were also able to purchase and rent homes without being restricted to ghetto areas as the Issei had been.

The Issei's productive years were now coming to an end, and it was time for the Nisei to take care of their parents. My own parents came east from Salt Lake City to live with my sister and me. We spent a year in Philadelphia where I taught in a small Quaker school and was accepted with warmth by the children, their parents, and my colleagues. My father found work in the shipping department of a church board and became one of their best packers.

We eventually moved to New York City, where my sister became a teacher in a private nursery school and I worked as a secretary. My father, however, had difficulty finding work. A friend found a job for him in a factory painting flowers on glassware, but in spite of his enthusiasm in this totally unfamiliar milieu, he was dismissed after a few days because he lacked the proper skills. It was the first time in his entire life that he had been dismissed from a job, but with his usual sense of humor, he recounted the experience to his friends with amusement rather than rancor.

Like most Issei, my parents missed the mild climate of California and found it depressing to be confined in our dark three-room apartment. My father, especially, longed for a house and a garden where he could again enjoy growing things. My parents finally returned to California and lived for a time in two small rooms of "the Back House" at our old Japanese church in Oakland, which had been converted, as were several other Japanese churches, into a temporary hostel for returning Japanese Americans.

My father had lost virtually all of his retirement benefits at the now defunct Mitsui and Company, but he had not lost his spirit or vitality. He was determined and eager to begin a new life, and my mother, although her health was deteriorating, was ready to begin with him.

In May 1949 my father filed three "Claims for Damage to or Loss of Real or Personal Property by a Person of Japanese Ancestry" in the names of my mother, my sister, and myself, making sure that the total amount did not exceed the limit, which he understood to be $2,500. My claim for my personal belongings and expenses related to the evacuation came to $1,037, and in June 1952 I was awarded the sum of $386.25, the bulk of which I sent to my parents. Although the Japanese Americans suffered losses estimated by the Federal Reserve Bank to have been roughly $400 million, the average award for some 23,000 claimants was only $440.

Following his return to California, my father worked for a young friend, assisting him in a fledgling import-export business. When that failed, he worked for another friend in the dry cleaning business, where he sometimes even mended clothes. It was on the basis of his meager salary at this last job, rather than on his salary at Mitsui, that his social security benefits were determined for the remainder of his life. My mother's benefits came to about $30 a month, and she cherished that small amount as "a gift from the government," using it carefully for special occasions and for money orders to supplement the dozens of packages my parents sent to friends and relatives in Japan for many years following the war.

A postwar reunion with my grandmother on her
eighty-eighth birthday. Los Angeles, 1950.

In 1951, almost ten years after their lives had been decimated by the war and their forced removal, my parents were able to purchase a house with the help of my sister, who left New York City to live with them and work at the YWCA in Oakland as program director. The house was just two blocks from the one they first rented in 1917, but this time no one came to ask them to leave. My sister stayed with them a year and then left for Connecticut to marry a professor of mathematics at Yale University.

In the meantime, I spent two years in Japan as a Ford Foundation Foreign Area Fellow and became acquainted with the relatives and friends who until then had been only strangers to me. I often surprised and amused them by using old-fashioned Japanese words and phrases taught me by my Meiji Era parents, who had also instilled in me values and thoughts far more traditional than those held by some of my Japanese contemporaries.

I climbed to remote wooded temple cemeteries to pour water on the tombstones of my grandfathers and maternal grandmother "to refresh their spirits," and I traveled the countryside, finding it incredibly beautiful. Although I went primarily as a writer to collect more folktales, I became equally immersed in the magnificent arts and crafts of Japan. The strength and honesty of its folk art especially appealed to me, and I felt an immediate kinship with the Japanese craftsmen I met. I was privileged to become acquainted with the three founders of the Mingei (folk art) movement in Japan—the philosopher-writer Soetsu Yanagi, and the noted potters Shoji Hamada and Kanjiro Kawai. Their Zen-oriented philosophy, their wholeness of spirit, and their totality as human beings enriched me immeasurably and made a lasting impact on my thought and writing.

My experience in Japan was as positive and restorative as the evacuation had been negative and depleting. I came home aware of a new dimension to myself as a Japanese American and with new respect and admiration for the culture that had made my parents what they were. The circle was complete. I feel grateful today for the Japanese values and traditions they instilled in me and kept alive in our home, and unlike the days of my youth, I am proud to be a Japanese American and am secure in that knowledge of myself.

I returned from Japan not knowing how long I would remain with my parents, but stayed to care for them in their declining years and to give them what comfort and sustenance I could.

In his seventy-sixth year my father suffered a stroke that left him partially paralyzed. But in the remaining ten years of his life, he learned to write with his left hand, continued to correspond with many friends, and did not abandon his annual campaign to raise funds for Doshisha University's Department of Theology, which his Issei friends supported generously. He and my mother faithfully attended Sycamore Congregational Church each Sunday, and joined its members in a fund-raising drive that enabled the church to build a new sanctuary only sixteen years after the Japanese Americans returned from the camps to begin their new lives in California. When my mother died in 1967, my father endured her death with more strength than my sister or I. He had helped so many families through so many deaths, he knew what had to be done, and from his wheelchair he quietly and resolutely made all the necessary decisions.

My parents, like many of their Issei friends, did not fear death, for they had faced it so often and accepted it as a part of life. Both of them planned their own funeral services long before their deaths, selecting their favorite Japanese hymns and Bible verses. My mother wanted only a small family funeral and a memorial service for her friends, but my father wanted the customary evening funeral service held for most Issei. We followed both their wishes.

The wartime evacuation of the Japanese Americans has already been well documented in many fine scholarly books. My story is a very personal one, and I speak only for myself and of those Issei and Nisei who were in the realm of my own experience, aware that they are only a small part of a larger whole. The story of my family is not typical of all Japanese immigrant families, and the lives of many other Japanese Americans were undoubtedly touched with more wartime tragedy and heartache than my own.

Still, there are many young Americans who have never heard about the evacuation or known of its effect on one Japanese American family. I hope the details of the life of my family, when added to those of others, will enhance their understanding of the history of the Japanese in California and enable them to see it as a vital element in that glorious and complex story of the immigrants from all lands who made America their home.

If my story has been long in coming, it is not because I did not want to remember our incarceration or to make this interior journey into my earlier self, but because it took so many years for these words to find a home. I am grateful that at last they have.

Today as a writer of books for young people, I often speak at schools about my experiences as a Japanese American. I want the children to perceive me not as a foreigner, as some still do, or as the stereotypic Asian they often see on film and television, but as a human being. I tell them of my pride in being a Japanese American today, but I also tell them I celebrate our common humanity, for I feel we must never lose our sense of connection with the human race. I tell them how it was to grow up as a Japanese American in California. I tell them about the Issei who persevered in a land that denied them so much. I tell them how our own country incarcerated us—its citizens—during World War II, causing us to lose that most precious of all possessions, our freedom.

The children ask me many questions, most of them about my wartime experiences. "I never knew we had concentration camps in America," one child told me in astonishment. "I thought they were only in Germany and Russia."

And so the story of the wartime incarceration of the Japanese Americans, as painful as it may be to hear, needs to be told and retold and never forgotten by succeeding generations of Americans.

I always ask the children why they think I wrote *Journey to Topaz* and *Journey Home,* in which I tell of the wartime experiences of the Japanese Americans. "To tell about the camps?" they ask. "To tell how you felt? To tell what happened to the Japanese people?"

"Yes," I answer, but I continue the discussion until finally one of them will say, "You wrote those books so it won't ever happen again."

And that is why I wrote this book. I wrote it for the young Japanese Americans who seek a sense of continuity with their past. But I wrote it as well for all Americans, with the hope that through knowledge of the past, they will never allow another group of people in America to be sent into a desert exile ever again.